Columbia University

Contributions to Education

Teachers College Series

No. 633

AMS PRESS
NEW YORK

AN EXPERIMENTAL APPLICATION
OF A
PHILOSOPHY OF SCIENCE TEACHING
IN AN ELEMENTARY SCHOOL

By
George W. Haupt, Ph.D.

TEACHERS COLLEGE, COLUMBIA UNIVERSITY
CONTRIBUTIONS TO EDUCATION, NO. 633

BUREAU OF PUBLICATIONS
Teachers College, Columbia University
NEW YORK CITY
1935

Library of Congress Cataloging in Publication Data

Haupt, George Webster, 1900-
   An experimental application of a philosophy of
science teaching in an elementary school.

   Reprint of the 1935 ed., issued in series: Teachers
College, Columbia University. Contributions to
education, no. 633.
   Originally presented as the author's thesis, Columbia.
   Bibliography: p.
   1. Science--Study and teaching (Elementary)
I. Title. II. Series: Columbia University. Teachers
College. Contributions to education, no. 633.
LB1585.H35 1972   372.3'5'044   75-176848
ISBN 0-404-55633-7

Reprinted by Special Arrangement with Teachers
College Press, New York, New York

From the edition of 1935, New York
First AMS edition published in 1972
Manufactured in the United States

AMS PRESS, INC.
NEW YORK, N. Y.   10003

Acknowledgments

THE author wishes to express his gratitude to the members of his dissertation committee, Professors H. B. Bruner, G. S. Craig, S. R. Powers, Rollo G. Reynolds, and R. B. Spence for their unfailing help. To Professors Craig and Powers, especially, he feels greatly indebted for guidance, invaluable assistance, and the opportunities and facilities which were made available by them.

This study would have been impossible without the coöperation of Professor Rollo G. Reynolds and the staff of the Horace Mann Elementary School, and the author thanks them sincerely.

He also wishes to thank Professor F. L. Fitzpatrick for his analysis of the data and judgments on their classification, and Professor Paul R. Hanna for suggestions concerning the presentation of material.

The author is deeply indebted to those student-teachers in the department of Natural Sciences of Teachers College who aided in the testing programs and who contributed materials from their schools.

G. W. H.

Contents

CHAPTER I

The Purpose of the Study Determined from Issues in a Confused Field

IF SCIENCE instruction in the elementary school is to grow and become more firmly established, it would seem that it should profit from a clearly defined and generally accepted purpose and philosophy. A survey of the writings of authorities in the field reveals that there are formulations of purposes and philosophies but that there is disparity among them. Differences in opinion are always valuable, and they are especially needed during the formative stages of a movement or growth, but there should be constant effort toward an adjustment of differing points of view based upon inquiry and research.

This study is an attempt to furnish objective data bearing on some questions suggested by differences of opinion and of points of view held by leaders in the field of science instruction in the elementary school.

As a background for perhaps a fuller interpretation of the field in general and of this study in particular, there is given a summary of an analysis of the writings of those who have influenced science instruction notably in the elementary school. An analysis of the writings from these sources establishes the following questions upon which there is not only lack of agreement but, in some cases, quite opposing positions:

I. What are the objectives and aims for science instruction in the elementary school and how shall these be stated?

II. What values are desired from elementary school science?

III. From what fields of science shall the content be taken?

IV. Shall personification and animism be used for motivation?

V. Upon what psychological assumptions shall proposals for selection and gradation of content be based?

The positions taken on these questions will be illustrated with pertinent quotations.

I. WHAT ARE THE OBJECTIVES AND AIMS FOR SCIENCE
INSTRUCTION IN THE ELEMENTARY SCHOOL AND
HOW SHALL THEY BE STATED?

The points of view and types of formulation of objectives and aims for science instruction can be classified into two groups: (1) objectives stated as of moral, ethical, civic, vocational, aesthetic, and spiritual value, and (2) objectives stated as broad conceptions, or "generalizations," indicative of content to be taught or learned.

Objectives of Moral, Ethical, Civic, Vocational, Aesthetic, and Spiritual Value

In the lower grades the dominant purpose shall be the aesthetic; in the upper grades the dominant purpose shall be the economic and social.[1]

We are to open the child's mind to his natural existence, develop his sense of responsibility and of self-dependence, train him to respect the resources of the earth, teach him the obligations of citizenship, interest him sympathetically in the occupations of men, quicken his relations to human life in general, and touch his imagination with the spiritual forces of the world.[2]

To briefly summarize, then, our task seems to be: (a) to impart (knowledge, power); (b) to train (sense perception, thinking, judgment, imagination, expression); (c) to develop (the sense of right and truth, the sense of the beautiful, higher ideals, character). Let us keep these things in mind in developing our method.[3]

In basing a plan of nature study upon its human values it may be necessary to explain what is meant by the worth of the study in the curriculum. Throughout all the details of the various kinds of values we shall discuss, the paramount value to be aimed at is *character, will to do good, power to create happiness*. No lesson that does not contribute toward this end can claim the right to a place in the course.[4]

Aims and Objectives for the Teaching of Nature Study and
Elementary Science[5]

A. Ethical Aim
   3. Desire to follow the truth—moral uprightness.
B. Spiritual Aim
   6. Sense of companionship with outdoor life, and abiding love of nature.
C. Aesthetic Aim
   11. Ability to create beauty and to use it.

[1] Trafton, G. H., *The Teaching of Science in the Elementary School*, p. 196.
[2] Bailey, L. H., *The Nature Study Idea*, p. 11.
[3] Munson, J. P., *Education Through Nature Study*, p. 86.
[4] Hodge, C. F., *Nature Study and Life*, p. 17.
[5] Department of Superintendence, *Fourth Yearbook*, "The Nation at Work on the Public School Curriculum," pp. 66-70.

D. Intellectual Aim
   19. Development of poise and common sense.
E. Social Aim
   39. Sincerity, honesty, straightforwardness, truthfulness, fairdealing, steadfastness, and reliability in one's dealings with others.
F. Civic Aim
   49. Ability to discern the social obligations and individual rights of one's self and others.
G. Economic Aim
   53. Reduction of cost of living through gardening.
H. Vital Aim
   56. Ability to protect one's self from microörganisms and poisons from plants, venomous snakes, etc., and to deal with them and their products effectively in case of attack.
I. Avocational Aim
   63. Ability to utilize music for a helpful, abundant, and varied awakening of one's emotional nature.
J. Vocational Aim
   68. Ability to supplement one's income.
K. Practical Aim
   70. Ability to make use of the forces of nature and science for personal betterment.[6]

Objectives Stated as Broad Conceptions, or "Generalizations,"[7] Indicative of Content

We must seek then, some unifying idea in nature study sufficiently complex to insure an increasing difficulty commensurate with the increasing power of the pupils.[8]

The writer knows from his own experience as a student, that many teachers of advanced science are failures, as teachers, because they do not arouse in the student's mind those great conceptions which give meaning to things observed by the student, and add that intellectual interest which makes arduous work a pleasure. Sentimental appreciation is a poor substitute for that intellectual pleasure which arises from the discovery of truths, revealing themselves as connecting links between the known and the unknown.[9]

Because of the immaturity of the child, however, there is an unique need in elementary school science for specific statements of the meanings to be developed in each grade and also of the broader scientific principles or generalizations toward a later understanding of which the attainment of these specific goals contributes. The failure to include these larger generalizations

---

[6] Each of the above eleven aims heads a list of sub-aims, varying in number from one, for K, to twenty-one, for D. There are seventy sub-aims in all. One illustrative sub-aim is given for each aim.

[7] See pages 98-100 of this study.

[8] Downing, E. R., in *Nature Study Review*, Vol. 3, p. 194, 1907.

[9] Munson, J. P., *op. cit.*, pp. 71-72.

as larger objectives has prevented the integration of the work in the different grades.[10]

In a program of general education which is for the most part the work of the public schools, the work of instruction will be directed toward accomplishment of understanding of those principles and generalizations of science that have largest application.[11]

It should be noted that . . . the subject matter is not the only end in the science program. Attitudes, appreciations, and skills will be concomitant with the development of many of these meanings.[12]

At this point we may summarize the discussion by saying that certain new principles and conceptions have profoundly influenced the thinking of educated people who are in no sense scientists or specialists. As such, the educated layman cannot afford to be ignorant of them. A few of these are:

The sun is the chief source of the energy for the earth.

The universe, including the earth, is very old. The surface of the earth has not always had its present appearance and is constantly changing.

Space is vast.

Present conditions are apt to persist a very long time on the earth. No catastrophe for the entire earth is probable for immense periods of time.

Species have survived because by adaptations and adjustments they have become fitted to the conditions under which they live.[13]

II. WHAT VALUES ARE DESIRED FROM ELEMENTARY SCHOOL SCIENCE?

There is agreement that the pupil shall *observe, identify,* and *collect,* but a number of writers specify that these activities shall be conducted as means to *interpretation* rather than as ends in themselves. (One contributor holds "poetic interpretation" to be of greater importance than "scientific interpretation.")

Observation, Identification, and Collecting as Ends

In the primary grades the chief thing to emphasize is identification.[14]

I may summarize the distinction between nature study and science as now held by the most active workers in nature study as follows: Nature study is primarily the simple observational study of common natural objects and processes for the sake of personal acquaintance with the things which appeal to human interest directly and independently of relations of organized science.[15]

[10] Craig, G. S., *Certain Techniques Used in Developing a Course of Study in Science for the Horace Mann Elementary School,* p. 4.
[11] Powers, S. R., in *Teachers College Record,* Vol. 32, p. 20, 1930.
[12] Craig, G. S., *op. cit.,* p. 7.
[13] Craig, G. S., in *Child Study,* Vol. 6, p. 209, 1929.
[14] Trafton, G. H., *op. cit.,* p. 99.
[15] Bigelow, M. A., in *Nature Study Review,* Vol. 3, p. 4, 1907.

Observation, Identification, and Collecting as Means to Other Values

But true science work does not stop with mere seeing, hearing, or feeling; it not only furnishes a mental picture as a basis for reasoning but it includes an interpretation of what has been received through the senses. A child and a goat may see the same thing, with the advantages of vision on the side of the goat; but the latter has no power to interpret what he sees and is, therefore, essentially non-scientific. In these early interpretations, lie the beginnings of the reasoning power, and with its development comes self-reliance, independence of thought, and a general strength of character which makes a man among men. If a pupil be permitted to carefully examine an object or a set of conditions, and then be required to interpret what he sees, he is from that moment ever after stronger than he was before. By that act, no matter how trivial, he begins the great work of self-emancipation from the rule of chance in so far as his interpretation has taught him how the forces about him may be resisted, guided, and controlled.[16]

It is a fact of tremendous import for teachers to remember that there can be no rational observation of anything that is not stimulated and guided by the suggestion of law. Failure to understand the importance of this point is responsible for the unspeakable confusion which now exists in most teachers' minds regarding the selection and presentation of material in nature study. The examination by children into the minute details of a subject is not only a physical impossibility, but it is also an absurdity, for the simple reason that for them through these minutiae there can be no manifestation of law. Illustrations are abundant. The older botany, when tried with the children, failed for precisely this reason. The children could see, physically, the venation, margin, shape, etc., of leaves; but their work fell below true observation, and consequently interest died out, because as presented, no reason or law suggested itself in explanation of these facts. When the same facts are reached through a broad presentation of the plant's relations to light, heat, and moisture, they at once become true and interesting objects of observation and fruitful sources of thought, because the perceived relationships suggest reasons that explain them. The same is true whatever may be the aspect of presentation—that of beauty as well as that of use. For the idea of beauty rests finally upon the perception of fitness, of adaptation; and adaptation points to the statement of a law.[17]

In accordance with the modern interpretation the child should be taught in science to observe and reason about those things in school which it is desirable for him to observe and reason about in actual life. The use of the power of observation is a method by which science is taught, but the training of the power should not be the aim. It is a means, and not an end.[18]

---

[16] Jackman, W. S., *Nature Study for the Common Schools*, pp. 2-3.
[17] Jackman, W. S., in *Third Yearbook of the National Society for the Study of Education*, Part II, p. 10, 1904.
[18] Trafton, G. H., *op. cit.*, p. 16.

Collecting should be an incident, particularly with very young children, and it should be encouraged only when it has some definite purpose.[19]

Would you tell the child the names of the things? Certainly, the same as I should tell him the name of a new boy or girl. But I should not stop with the name. Nature study does not ask finally, "What is the thing?", but "How does the thing live?" or "What does it do?" or "How did it get here?" or "What can I do with it?" The name is only a part of the language that enables us to talk about the object. Tell the name at the outset and have the matter done with. Then go on to questions.[20]

Should identification be an end in itself in the elementary school? The point of view which is accepted tentatively in the construction of the Horace Mann course of study in Elementary Science is that instruction in knowing plants, animals, rocks, and stars by name need not be an end in itself. Identification may become an integral part of developing important meanings about plants, animals, rocks, and stars.[21]

The Position Relative to "Poetic Interpretation"

I plead only that the poetic interpretation is allowable.[22]

We cannot say that the good poets have not known nature, because they have not interpreted by fact alone. Have they not left us the essence and flavor of the fields and the woods and the sky? And yet they were not scientists. So different are these types of interpretation that we all unconsciously set the poet over against the scientist.[23]

III. FROM WHAT FIELDS OF SCIENCE SHALL THE CONTENT BE TAKEN?

One group of authorities states that all physical and chemical phenomena shall be excluded from the content, with perhaps some physical science included in the upper grade levels of the elementary school. Another group states that content from all fields of science shall receive attention on all grade levels.

Content Chiefly from the Biological Sciences

The topics for the primary grades shall deal largely with the study of plants and animals; the work for upper grades should cover all phases of elementary science.[24]

The biological, geological, astronomical, and meteorological aspects of nature, as differentiated from the physical and chemical aspects of environ-

---

[19] Bailey, L. H., *op. cit.*, p. 195.
[20] *Op. cit.*, p. 196.
[21] Craig, G. S., *Certain Techniques Used in Developing a Course of Study in Science for the Horace Mann Elementary School*, p. 27.
[22] Bailey, L. H., *op. cit.*, p. 37.
[23] *Op. cit.*, p. 35.
[24] Trafton, G. H., *op. cit.*, p. 196.

ment, natural and man-made, command the greatest attention in nature study and elementary science courses.[25]

The more I study the problem, the more it seems to me that this side of nature (plants and animals) is the sheet anchor of elementary education, all the more necessary as modern life tends to drift away from nature into artificialities of every sort.[26]

Content from All Fields of Science

Animal, plant, mineral, river, cloud, sunbeam, mountain, physical, and chemical changes are all matters of equal and absorbing interest to him, and if left to himself he will inquire as freely about one as another. It is a mistaken idea that the child's interest is best aroused by a "thorough" study of a few living things, animals, or plants, such as form the chief stock-in-trade in many schoolrooms.[27]

When we claim that physics cannot be taught to children we disagree with Faraday and perhaps show that we do not properly understand either physics or children.[28]

It is most important that the material selected to go into the course of study for each grade be balanced to include the elements of learning which represent a rich experience in this field. Each grade level should give the child some opportunity for growth in the five great major fields of science, astronomy, biology, chemistry, geology, and physics. This cannot be accomplished by studying only plants and animals.[29]

IV. SHALL PERSONIFICATION AND ANIMISM BE USED FOR MOTIVATION?

There is expression for and against the use of personification and animism for motivation.

Use Personification and Animism

There are two ways of interpreting nature—the way of fact and the way of fancy. To the scientist and to the average man the interpretation by fact is usually the only admissible one. He may not be open to argument or conviction that there can be any other truthful way of knowing the external world. Yet, the artist and the poet know this world and they do not know it by cold knowledge or by analysis. It appeals to them in its moods. Yet it is as real to them as to the analyst. Too much are we of this generation tied to mere phenomena. We have a right to a poetic interpretation of nature. The child interprets nature and the world through imagination and feeling and sympathy. Note the intent and sympathetic face as the child watches the

25 In *Fourth Yearbook of the Department of Superintendence*, p. 65, 1926.
26 Hodge, C. F., *op. cit.*, Preface, p. vii.
27 Jackman, W. S., *Nature Study for the Common Schools*, Preface, p. iii.
28 Woodhull, J. F., in *Nature Study Review*, Vol. 6, p. 7, 1910.
29 Craig, G. S., in *Child Study*, Vol. 6, p. 210, 1929.

ant carrying its grains of sand, and pictures to itself the home and the bed and the kitchens and the sisters and the school that comprise the ant's life. What does the flower think? Who are the little people that teeter and swing in the sunbeam? What is the brook saying as it rolls over the pebbles? Why is the wind so sorrowful as it moans on the house corners in the dull November days? There are leaves whispering in the trees, and there are chariots of fire rolling on the long, low clouds at twilight. Wherever it may look, the young mind is impressed with the mystery of the unknown. The child looks out to nature with great eyes of wonder.[30]

Do Not Use Personification and Animism

Many teachers realizing the lack of this element [imagination] in nature study, have sought to supply it by treating all individuals under the guise of human beings. There is nothing in nature, from a raindrop to an oyster, that has not been personified in the hope that this personal relationship may be brought out a little stronger. The general effect of this plan reminds one of the grotesqueness of the hand-organ monkey that is dressed up in a red coat and a cocked hat. His ill-fitting garments certainly add nothing to his character as a monkey, and they fail to give him anything of the bearing and dignity of a man.[31]

Many nature writers for children have insisted on mixing their own sentiments with science. We have been deluged with pseudo-nature material. Apparently this movement is due to the entrance into this field of many people who know little or nothing about children or about science. There is no need of sugar-coating science with myths and fairy tales. Science is truth, as near as man can get to the truth at any given time, and it should not be mixed with untruths. Myths and fairy tales should be taught as myths and fairy tales, and not as science. Present studies indicate that children have little desire for the sugar-coated substitute for science.[32]

V. UPON WHAT PSYCHOLOGICAL ASSUMPTIONS SHALL PROPOSALS FOR SELECTION AND GRADATION OF CONTENT BE BASED?

There is agreement that science in the elementary school must conform to principles of psychology, but there are differences in the psychological assumptions which are held. A "saltatory, culture epoch" psychology seems to be definitely in mind by one group of writers; a "continuous, unfolding" psychology by another.

Illustrative of the Expression for a Recognition of the Psychology of Learning

The proper clew which will enable the teacher to determine upon the prin-

[30] Bailey, L. H., op. cit., p. 35.
[31] Jackman, W. S., in Third Yearbook of the National Society for the Study of Education, Part II, pp. 44-45, 1904.
[32] Craig, G. S., op. cit., Vol. 6, p. 210, 1929.

ciples which must guide him in his method of instruction in elementary science, must come, therefore, from a close study of the child.[33]

Nature study must be organized and adjusted to the established principles of elementary education. It cannot permanently continue to ignore these principles.[34]

It [nature study] is regarded as a movement to relate education to daily life, to make education a part of life instead of something apart from life. It seeks to accomplish this end by a wise training of the senses, using for its material the natural objects or phenomena surrounding the child. This training of the external organs of relation, if properly done, involves a knowledge of the development of the child mind in order that successive steps may follow in a perfectly natural and, therefore, perfectly logical sequence.[35]

In nature study as in everything else, the work must begin with what the individual has already acquired, and it should proceed from this according to the natural laws of mind growth.[36]

We must recognize the established principles of child study in all our nature study for elementary education. To the general recognition of this great principle we owe the comparatively recent decided advances in differentiating between nature study for elementary schools and nature study for higher schools.[37]

Illustrative of a "Saltatory, Culture Epoch" Psychology

It has been said that the child is a young savage. This is true in several respects. Science tells us that an animal or a plant in its physical development passes, in general, through the stages through which the race to which it belongs has passed in its development. For example, in the embryology of the frog there is a stage that is like the fish—the tadpole stage. Other facts prove the origin of frogs from fish-like ancestors. Every frog repeats this fish-like stage. It has become an educational maxim that the mental evolution of a child corresponds in a measure to the mental evolution of the race to which he belongs. That is, the child exhibits mental traits that were once characteristic of his race when in the primitive state. In pedagogy we hear this spoken of as the Culture Epoch Theory, and though it is not fully worked out in its applications, this theory is already useful in education. We cannot safely change the course of nature in the development of mind or body. It is better to take a suggestion from nature and to work with, rather than against, her.[38]

Of first importance is the fact that man's primitive relations to nature are mainly biological—relations to animal and plant life. [Then follows the phases to teach in the order given.]

[33] Jackman, W. S., *op. cit.*, p. 8.
[34] Bigelow, M. A., in *Nature Study Review*, Vol. 11, p. 410, 1915.
[35] Coulter, S., in *Nature Study Review*, Vol. 4, p. 11, 1908.
[36] Jackman, W. S., *op. cit.*, Part II, p. 9, 1904.
[37] Bigelow, M. A., in *Nature Study Review*, Vol. 3, p. 6, 1907.
[38] Holtz, F. L., *Nature Study*, p. 10.

Subjugation of Animals
Dominion Over Animals
Cultivation of Plants.[39]

Another principle solidly established and here utilized, is that interest in life forms precedes that in inanimate nature for children of the ages here in view (Grades I to IX). Rock forms, crystals, stars, weather, and seasons are all interesting, but have their nascent period later, and at this stage pale before the deep, instinctive love of pets and the fauna and flora of the immediate environment.[40]

But the childhood of the race was very long, and we should not wish to force its period, brief at best, in the life of the individual. The weathering of rock and the formation of soil afford interesting lessons in modern geology; but men dug and planted, and established fruitful relations with Mother Earth thousands of years before geology was ever dreamed of. So with combustion and the various forms of water; why not let the children wonder about them for a few years, and then come with interest keen and fresh to their study in the chemistry and physics of the high school or college?[41]

Sense stimulation gives rise to unconscious induction. Much of the nature study work in the lower grades must be of this nature. Observation must here predominate. Indeed it is doubtful if any considerable effort should here be made by the teacher to lead the pupil to generalize. The history of the human race, so far as we have any record of that history, suggests that a period of unconscious induction preceded the age of generalization—the philosophical and the theological age—and that the latter ages preceded, in the history of western peoples at least, the period of conscious systematic study of nature—our present scientific age. The same stages properly belong to the individual: (1) the period of unconscious induction by a varied experience with natural things; (2) the period of generalization and speculation; (3) the scientific period, in which the individual, doubtful of his previous generalizations, yet impressed by their importance, proceeds voluntarily and systematically to test by accurate observation and experiment, the truth or absurdity of these previously formed general notions. This latter, alone, can be called science.[42]

Illustrative of a "Continuous, Unfolding" Psychology

There is now a demand for a continuous and correlated program of study. The new theory requires a curriculum in which learning experiences shall be arranged in such a manner that, as the child progresses through successive grades, he will have opportunity for continuous enlargement of his knowledge of the problems, principles, and generalizations that scholarly men find worthy of study. This new interpretation of the process of mental growth has now such general acceptance that it has determined the character of our

[39] Hodge, C. F., *op. cit.*, pp. 2-15.
[40] *Op. cit.*, Introduction, p. xiv, by G. S. Hall.
[41] *Op. cit.*, p. viii.
[42] Munson, J. P., *op. cit.*, pp. 63-64.

institutions for elementary and secondary education but it has not yet had full recognition in determining the objectives, content, and methods of the subjects of study.[43]

In nature study with children the teacher has to deal with untrained senses and with mental powers generally undeveloped. The pupil is unable either to see great detail or to grasp relationships that exist among the minutiae of the subject. As the story told by the pupil's senses is vague and inaccurate so the pictures of his incipient imagination are erratic and fanciful. He must, therefore, deal with larger masses than are necessary for the trained student of science. The sights must be more vivid, the weights heavier, the relations more striking, the movements more pronounced, and the functions more obvious. In natural science the better trained student discovers minute details and recognizes more delicate relations. It is upon these facts that a true system of gradation in nature study and science must rest. The attempt is usually made to establish grades by changing from one branch of the science to another and by the introduction of new and often unrelated subject matter.[44]

In recent years other school subjects have developed sequence and a plan providing for continuity through the elementary school grades, all of which has greatly increased the efficiency of instruction; but the general attitude regarding nature study has been quite different from that regarding other subjects.[45]

These excerpts show that very definite differences of opinion concerning content and method for science instruction in the elementary school are held by those whose writings have influenced the field.[46] There are differences of opinion concerning the very fundamental question of the type of aim and the manner of statement of the aim. Shall the aim be of the "moral, civic, ethical, and spiritual" type with statements of goals of attainment such as "moral uprightness," "ability to discern the social obligations and individual rights of one's self and others," etc.? Or shall it be the "generalization," or "objective," type with statements of goals of attainment such as "The universe including the earth is very old," "space is vast," "energy is not destroyed but is changed into other forms," etc.?

Shall the activities of observation, collecting, and identification be ends or means to explanations and interpretations?

[43] Powers, S. R., in *Thirty-First Yearbook of the National Society for the Study of Education*, Part I, pp. 5-6, 1932.

[44] Jackman, W. S., *op. cit.*, Part II, pp. 12-15, 1904.

[45] Craig, G. S., *Certain Techniques Used in Developing a Course of Study in Science for the Horace Mann Elementary School*, p. 2.

[46] While some of the foregoing excerpts were written as early as thirty years ago, the most recent courses of study show the prevailing influence of the points of view which they here illustrate.

Shall the science content for the elementary school be predominantly biological or shall it comprise content from all fields of science?

Shall or shall not personification and animism be used for motivation?

Shall grade placement be in terms of the special branches of science, biological for the lower grade levels and physical for the higher; or shall it be in terms of difficulty or complexity of content, irrespective of any special divisions of science?

These various points of view have become crystallized into two distinct philosophies of science instruction for children. On the one hand there is the proposal that experiences should be provided which permit of interpretation and explanation contributory to an understanding of "large generalizations." This philosophy is, of course, based on the assumption that children are capable of the kind of mental activity required by this type of aim. On the other hand there is the assumption that young children are not capable of the kind of mental activity necessitated by the "large generalization" type of aim and that therefore their experiences should consist mainly of observation. Just what are the types of mental activity necessitated by the employment of the "large generalization" type of aim? Are young children capable of these mental activities? It is to contribute objective data bearing upon these questions that this study is made.

CHAPTER II

Plan of the Study

THE purpose of this study, broadly stated, was to test the "objective" or "large generalization" type of aim in a teaching situation. Obviously, the first necessary step was to select an objective. The second step was to determine learning experiences, the interpretation of which would contribute to an understanding of the chosen objective. The third step was to present these contributory learning experiences and interpretations to children of six grades of an elementary school.

A discussion of the methods and sources of data used in the various stages of the study is given later, but they may be summarized here as follows:

I. The selection of a teaching objective. Chapter III.
    A. Review of related studies in the field of science education.
    B. Consideration of needs in science teaching.

II. Determination of elements of learning contributory to an understanding of the objective. Chapter IV.
    A. Selection of a concept suggestive of content contributory to an understanding of the objective.
    B. Analysis of books written by authorities for the non-specialist reader.
    C. Statements from children of Grades 1 to 6.

III. Pre-instructional testing of children of Grades 1 to 6. Chapter VI.

IV. Experimental teaching of children of Grades 1 to 6. Chapter VII.

V. Post-instructional testing of children of Grades 1 to 6. Chapter VI.

Analyses of the data are presented in Chapter VIII.

The discussion of the study, presented chiefly in Chapters V, IX, and X, is organized with a view to its bearing on the issues presented in Chapter I, as well as on several other questions which have recently been placed before the field in Part I of the *Thirty-First Yearbook of the National Society for the Study of Education*.[1] The latter points are indicated in the study.

It is hoped that this attempt at objective study will be a worthwhile addition to that necessary and valuable body of opinion and theory which has accumulated concerning the teaching of science, especially in the elementary school. As has been well said: "The psychology of a school subject should not be thought of as merely an attempt to apply deductively certain general conceptions derived from studies of mental development and learning. The newer psychology of the school subjects is not content with such deductive application but attacks directly the problems of learning in the subject by methods adapted to the study of these particular problems. Such direct study has contributed materially to our knowledge of learning in the subjects of reading, writing, and arithmetic, and this knowledge has been very influential in the organization of the curriculum and the determination of methods in these subjects. The same kind of direct study will doubtlessly prove equally productive in the study of the curriculum and methods in the other subjects, including science."[2]

[1] National Society for the Study of Education, *Thirty-First Yearbook*, Part I, A Program for Teaching Science, 1932.

[2] Freeman, F. N., "A Symposium on the Thirty-First Yearbook of the National Society for the Study of Education, Part I, entitled A Program for Teaching Science," *Science Education*, Vol. 16, No. 4, p. 305, April 1932.

CHAPTER III

Selection of a Teaching Objective

CRAIG[1] gives a list of major objectives or "large generalizations" which are evaluated according to their importance in contemporary life and thought. Several of the objectives of this list have since been subjected to further analytical study.

In one of these subsequent studies, Billig[2] has outlined content relative to the principle, or objective, "Living things survive because they are fitted to conditions under which they live and in which their structures and ways of living enable them to attain adult life and to leave offspring." This work was directed to the development of a professional course for prospective elementary school teachers and the experimental testing and teaching were done with students in a teacher-training course.

In another study, MacKay[3] arrayed learning elements contributory to the generalization, or objective: "Common non-living substances are reorganized by plants into substances which form the basis for the complex living material of plant and animal bodies; then, as the result of a series of changes, the complex materials are reduced to successively simpler substances until they become again common materials of the environment." The testing and teaching were done with ninth grade girls.

The objectives used in the above studies were considered with a view to their application to the requirement of this study, but it was decided to select an unexplored objective.

There has been discussion in the seminar in Science Education conducted in Teachers College of the possibility of resolving for curriculum purposes objectives having to do with the transformation and conservation of energy. It seems as though knowledge

[1] Craig, G. S., *Certain Techniques Used in Developing a Course of Study in Science for the Horace Mann Elementary School*, 1927.

[2] Billig, F. G., *A Technique for Developing Content for a Professional Course for Teachers in Elementary Schools*, 1930.

[3] MacKay, Minnette, *The Formation of a Generalization in the Minds of Ninth-Grade Biology Students*. Doctor's dissertation (manuscript) at Teachers College, Columbia University, New York. 1930.

contributory to such objectives is of significance and importance in education, both liberal and practical. The following is illustrative of statements which are being made by students in many different fields and which indicate the importance of the objectives mentioned:

> The laws expressing the relationship between energy and matter are, however, not solely of importance in pure science. They necessarily come first in order, in the fundamental sense described, in the whole record of human experience, and they control, in the last resort, the rise or fall of political systems, the freedom or bondage of nations, the movements of commerce and industry, the origin of wealth and poverty, and the general physical welfare of the race. If this has been too imperfectly recognized in the past, there is no excuse, now that these physical laws have become incorporated into everyday habits of thought, for neglecting to consider them first in questions relating to the future.[4]

Craig[5] has given some of the objectives pertaining to energy and its transformation an evaluation from two sources: (1) the educated laymen's judgment of needs and (2) the use of content involved in such objectives in answering children's questions. In a list of eighty-two objectives the educated laymen of Craig's study rank the following objectives thus:

Number 5. The sun as the source of energy and light.
Number 10. Matter and energy cannot be created or destroyed.
Number 32. The sources and uses of power.
Number 37. Chemical and physical change as a source of energy.
Number 56. The conversion of mechanical energy into electricity.
Number 68. Chemical and physical change as contrasted with annihilation.

From the standpoint of need in answering children's questions, out of the highest fifty classifications, the following objectives were ranked thus:

Number 7. The production, manifestations, and properties of electricity.
Number 30. The sun as the source of energy and light.
Number 46. The sources and uses of power.

It was decided to attempt a treatment of an objective having to do with the transformation of energy. This means that after formulating a statement concerning transformation of energy, a range of content would be selected for presentation in the first six grades of an elementary school which would permit of interpretations involved in the objective.

⁴ Soddy, F., *Matter and Energy*, pp. 10-11.
⁵ *Op. cit.*, pp. 21-24; 41-42.

The "energy objective" may seem at first thought a difficult selection for the elementary school, but elementary school teachers constantly present to their pupils content, particularly in the study of plants, whose interpretations can be made in terms of energy transfer. The data of this study show some of the places where such interpretations can be made (and to what extent successfully made in this case), but one illustration may here be suggested. Elementary school teachers have their children plant bulbs, collect and press leaves, note the shape, margin, veins, and arrangement of leaves, etc. But what can these activities mean to the children unless there is interpretation? And is not in the meaning of the plant's relation to light a fundamental interpretation involved?[6] Perhaps the "energy objectives" have a distinct place in the elementary school.

However, for such to be the case, attainment of the objective need not necessarily be accomplished.[7] The objective "Green plants convert the energy of light into the energy of food and fuel" may be held by teachers on all six grade levels but attainment of the objective accomplished on none of them. Yet, the objective can have a place in the elementary school (1) if something contributory to the objective can be learned on each of the six grade levels, and (2) if there is growth in the approach to understanding of the objective on ascending grade levels.

This point is of considerable importance and will be discussed and illustrated throughout the study. The question, What will be the difference in practice on successive grade levels? is frequently asked concerning the use of the major generalization as an objective throughout a range of grades. "The natural implication . . . is that the various principles shall be explicitly stated in the course of instruction at successive grade levels. If this is done, some way will have to be found to make it appear that the later treatment of a generalization really adds something to the earlier treatment and is not mere idle repetition."[8]

Further, the same objective may be held by teachers on the junior high school level and the senior high school level with increasing enlargement with advance in grade level. On these

[6] See the statement by W. S. Jackman on page 5 of this study.

[7] See pages 98-100 of this study.

[8] Freeman, F. N., "A Symposium on the Thirty-First Yearbook of the National Society for the Study of Education, Part I, entitled, A Program for Teaching Science." *Science Education*, Vol. 16, No. 4, p. 304, April 1932.

higher grade levels the question of enlargement of general understanding of an objective is not the only one involved. Somewhere
in these higher grade ranges will come the beginning of specialization. It is suggested that further study of this particular
objective on the junior and senior high school levels would yield
evidence bearing upon "the fundamental problem that is involved
in the union of specialization and the attainment of broad generalizations."[9]

[9] Freeman, F. N., in *Thirty-First Yearbook of the National Society for the Study of Education*, Part I, p. 347.

CHAPTER IV

Determination of Elements of Learning Contributory to the Objective

HAVING chosen to present content pertaining to an understanding of conservation and transformation of energy, it was necessary to determine something of the nature and extent of such content.

Some techniques[1] are available for use in determining content or elements of learning contributory to the understanding of objectives. These consist of (1) an evaluation and selection of books concerning the objective written by authorities for the non-specialist reader and (2) from the books selected, an excerption of statements pertaining to the objective.

It seemed that an immediate application of these techniques to this study could be made, but when an analysis of books was begun in order to determine what was said concerning the "transformation and conservation of energy," it was discovered that there were two types of statements: (1) statements of a general nature relative to energy; (2) statements concerning various specific manifestations of energy, e.g., heat, electricity, light, magnetism, motion, etc.

Statements of a general nature such as "Our present mechanical civilization has been made possible through man's increasing control of energy and its transformations" tend to inculcate appreciations and might even be useful as objectives, but the learning of statements of this type does not greatly help to develop a scientific conception of the transformation of energy. Such a conception must be built up or must emerge from learning experiences the explanation of which contribute to an understanding of the objective. For example, a scientific conception of the objective "The surface of the earth is constantly changing" would not result from

---

[1] Craig, G. S., *Certain Techniques Used in Developing a Course of Study for the Horace Mann Elementary School,* 1927.

Billig, F. G., *A Technique for Developing Content for a Professional Course for Teachers in Elementary Schools,* 1930.

MacKay, M., *The Formation of a Generalization in the Minds of Ninth Grade Biology Students.* Doctor's dissertation (manuscript) at Teachers College, Columbia University, New York, 1930.

the learning of such statements as "The earth did not always look as it does now," but would emerge from experiences with weathering, erosion, sedimentation, and the like.

The statements concerning heat, light, motion, electricity, etc., were more of the type desired, but it seemed that so many different manifestations of energy could not be treated in the manner contemplated. It was therefore decided to restrict the study to a special case of energy.

The two following criteria were formulated for guidance in this restriction:

A. The specific manifestation of energy selected for instruction in the elementary school should be one inherent in an extensive range of energy transformations.

B. The specific manifestation of energy selected for instruction in the elementary school should touch, to as great an extent as possible, the experiences of children of Grades 1 to 6.

Light was selected as presumably fulfilling these criteria most perfectly.

Having made this restriction, it was now thought that sources could be analyzed for statements concerning light and that from this analysis content and method for presentation of the objective would be revealed.

These sources were obtained from *The Book Review Digest*[2] for the years 1925 to 1929, inclusive, taking the title and author of every book dealing with *light* being listed. From this list only those books were retained whose authors were mentioned in *American Men of Science*.[3] After such selection the following books remained for analysis. (Analyses were included of two courses of study in science for the elementary school.)

Bazzoni, C. B., *Kernels of the Universe*, 1927.
Clarke, B. L., *Romance of Reality*, 1928.
Heyl, P. R., *Fundamental Concepts of Physics in the Light of Modern Discovery*, 1926.
Lewis, G. N., *Anatomy of Science*, 1927.
Newman, H. H., *Nature of the World and of Man*, 1926.
Slosson, E. E., *Snapshots of Science*, 1928.
Craig, G. S., *Tentative Course of Study in Elementary Science for Grades I-VI, Horace Mann School*, 1927.

[2] *The Book Review Digest.* The H. W. Wilson Company, 1925-1929.
[3] *American Men of Science.* The Science Press, 1927.

The Teaching of Nature Study and Elementary Science, The State of New Jersey, Department of Public Instruction, Trenton, New Jersey, July, 1929.

Although the purpose of the analysis of this selected list of sources was to obtain statements concerning light in its relation to energy, it was thought worth while to excerpt every statement which was made concerning light. By following this procedure, not only were elements of learning contributory to the chosen objective secured but also statements concerning other topics and phenomena. Thus the analysis revealed that these authorities used light in discussions of energy, the heavenly bodies, phototropisms and adaptations of life to light, and the relation of light to sickness and health. It also revealed what they evidently considered of value for the non-specialist reader concerning the nature, manifestations, and properties of light.

The statements concerning light from these sources were recorded on cards as shown in the sample below.

	N. J.	H. M.	Clarke	Bazzoni	Heyl	Lewis	Newman	Slosson
Sunlight is the power that is used in the plant factory.	45		166					

Thus the statement "Sunlight is the power that is used in the plant factory" (or a statement implying so precisely the same thought that distinction would be superfluous) is found on page 45 of the *Horace Mann Course of Study* and on page 166 of Clarke's *Romance of Reality.*

An outline of the results which the analysis yielded is given on page 22.

It is now seen that from the analysis of these discussions of light there were obtained some statements or elements of learning pertaining to the energy objective. It is also seen that in discussing light in its relation to energy the transformations presented by these writers involved three phenomena, namely, electricity, life, and chemical action. There is also some quantitative indication of the relative importance (for the non-specialist reader) of these three phases of the transformation of energy, for from these

RESULTS OF THE ANALYSIS OF AUTHORITATIVE SOURCES
AND COURSES OF STUDY

319 Distinct Elements.   *Frequency of 513*

	No. of Elements	Frequency
I. *Light in Relation to Energy, Its Transformations and Conservation.*	63	92
A. General. Unclassified.	9	18
B. Electricity	1	1
1. Electricity produces heat.	1	1
C. Life	39	54
1. Relation of light to plant growth and metabolism	35	46
2. Effects of products of plant growth and metabolism on animal metabolism	2	6
3. Animal metabolism produces light.	2	2
D. Chemical action	14	19
1. Light produces chemical action. .	8	12
2. Chemical action produces heat and light.	6	7
II. *Light in Relation to the Heavenly Bodies.*	15	35
A. General. Unclassified.	7	20
B. The sun	7	14
C. The seasons	1	1
III. *The Nature, Manifestations, and Properties of Light*	173	300
A. General. Unclassified.	11	16
B. How light is made	40	63
C. The properties of light	28	50
D. How light is distributed	27	53
E. The speed of light	32	55
F. Reflection of light	4	4
G. Refraction of light	9	18
H. Dispersion	15	30
I. Transparency, translucency, and opacity	7	11
IV. *Natural and Artificial Light*	1	1
A. Sources of artificial light	1	1
V. *Phototropism and Adaptations of Life to Light*	9	11
VI. *Relation of Light to Sickness and Health*	4	5
VII. *Appreciation of Light*	1	1
VIII. *Unclassified*	53	68

authorities there were secured thirty-nine different statements concerning the relation of light to life, fourteen different statements concerning the relation of light to chemical action, and one statement concerning the relation of light to electricity.

This array and organization of statements pertaining to the energy objective were then considered with a view to their incorporation into a teaching program. It appeared that this program could take one of two forms: (1) it could be organized so as to include all three of the phenomena or (2) it could be organized about only one of them. It seemed better to restrict attention to only one of the phenomena for the purposes of experimental instruction, and as there were more statements concerning the Light–Life phase it was tentatively selected.

The problem could now be more specifically defined. A conception of transformation of energy was to be approached through instruction which pertained to the energy relations between light and life.

Although there were now some elements of learning or statements at hand which could be used in organizing the instruction, it was thought that before instruction was begun it would be of value to know some of the ideas children held concerning light. It was believed that such information concerning children's experiences might be a source of content for the experimental teaching as well as a guide to its gradation. And further, it was believed that such information would give some indication of how well the Light–Life phase integrated with children's experiences in comparison with the other phases possible of selection.

As a means of determining some of the ideas which children held concerning the phenomena of light, the following letter was prepared:

To Coöperating Teachers and Principals:

We are making a study at the Horace Mann School of children's conceptions of the phenomena of LIGHT. You can help us by getting all of your children who write, from the first grade upward, to tell us all they can about light.

After placing the word LIGHT on the board, read or tell the following to the children: "Write, in the way you want to, all you can about light. All of you know many things about Light. Write these down as you think of them. If you have any trouble with the spelling of a word, spell it the way it sounds to you. Put your name, grade, and age at the top of each paper."

Do not allow the children to ask questions aloud for they may give suggestions to others. Please be sure to put the name, grade, and age at the top of each paper.

Return papers as soon as convenient to

G. W. Haupt
Horace Mann School
Teachers College

This letter was distributed to elementary school teachers and supervisors enrolled in the classes of the Department of Natural Sciences of Teachers College. Sixty-eight of these student-teachers returned one or more sets of children's papers (a "set" comprising the papers from one class of any of the six grade levels). In many cases in the lower grade levels, where the children could not write, the teachers wrote what the children told them. The total number of sets of papers returned was 162, the sets ranging from grades one to nine, inclusive. The statements from these children's papers were recorded and tabulated on cards, as shown in the sample.

Grade	I	II	III	IV	V	VI	VII
Without sunlight we would have no flowers or green plants	|		||||| |||||	||||| |||||	||||| ||||	||||| |||||	||||| |||||
			|		|		|
				|			

Thus the statement "Without sunlight we would have no flowers or green plants" (or a statement implying so precisely the same thought that distinction would be superfluous) occurred once in the papers of the first grade examined, six times in those of the third grade, eleven times in those of the fourth grade, nine times in those of the fifth grade, thirteen times in those of the sixth grade, and twelve times in those of the seventh grade.

The analysis which follows was made from 700 of these papers, 100 papers from each of Grades 1 to 7, inclusive.

RESULTS OF THE ANALYSIS OF CHILDREN'S PAPERS*

641 Distinct Elements.   Frequency of 4,003

	No. of Elements	Frequency
I. *Light in Relation to Energy, Its Transformations and Conservation*	150	1740
A. General. Unclassified.	11	69
B. Electricity	54	591
1. Chemical action makes electricity and light.	5	75
a. The electric cell		
2. Mechanical motion produces electricity.	14	37
3. Electricity produces mechanical motion.	1	1
4. Electricity produces heat and light.	29	471
a. The electric bulb		
b. The short circuit		
c. The arc light		
d. Lightning and aurora borealis..		
5. Light produces electricity.	1	1
6. Unclassified	4	6
C. Life	55	782
1. Relation of light to plant growth and metabolism	8	91
2. Products of plant growth and metabolism make heat and light.	22	379
a. Oils		
b. Gas		
3. Effect of products of plant growth and metabolism on animal metabolism	9	104
4. Animal metabolism produces light.	6	29
5. Products of animal metabolism produce light.	9	168
6. Light produces animal growth. ...	1	11
D. Mechanical motion	6	60
1. Mechanical motion produces heat and light.	6	60
2. See B 2 (Mechanical motion produces electricity).		
3. See B 3 (Electricity produces mechanical motion).		
E. Radio activity	5	31
1. Radio active substances give light.	5	31

* One hundred papers from each of Grades 1 to 7.

RESULTS OF THE ANALYSIS OF CHILDREN'S PAPERS (*Continued*)

	No. of Elements	Frequency
F. Chemical action ....,......	11	167
1. Light produces chemical action. ...	4	5
2. Chemical action produces heat and light.	7	162
3. Sêe B 1 (chemical action makes electricity and light).		
G. Heat	8	40
1. Light makes heat.	7	39
2. Heat makes light.	1	1
3. See B 4 (electricity produces heat and light).		
II. *Light in Relation to the Heavenly Bodies* ..	153	1024
A. The sun	39	366
1. General. Unclassified.	11	268
2. The nature of the sun	24	85
3. The nature of sunlight	4	13
B. The moon	23	245
1. General. Unclassified.	10	177
2. How the light of the moon is produced	9	61
3. The nature of the moon	3	6
4. The phases of the moon	1	1
C. The stars	13	140
1. General. Unclassified.	3	24
2. The nature of the stars	2	4
3. How starlight is produced	5	108
4. The distances of the stars	3	4
D. The planets	17	31
1. General. Unclassified.	8	16
2. How planets give light	9	15
E. Day and night	39	205
1. General. Unclassified.	1	1
2. The cause of day and night	38	204
F. Eclipses	6	14
1. General. Unclassified.	1	6
2. Cause of solar eclipses	3	6
3. Cause of lunar eclipse	2	2
G. The seasons	11	15
1. The cause of the seasons	11	15
H. General. Unclassified.	5	8
III. *The Nature, Manifestations and Properties of Light*	161	629
A. What light is	20	62
B. How light is made	10	58
C. The properties of light	23	38

RESULTS OF THE ANALYSIS OF CHILDREN'S PAPERS (*Concluded*)

	No. of Elements	Frequency
D. How light is distributed	2	3
E. The speed of light	26	63
F. Reflection of light	31	308
G. Refraction of light	5	5
H. Dispersion	5	6
I. Color	26	50
J. Transparency, translucency and opacity	6	19
K. Shadows	5	6
L. General. Unclassified.	2	11
IV. *Natural and Artificial Light*	59	229
A. Distinction between natural and artificial light	33	110
B. Uses of artificial light	26	119
V. *Thomas Edison and Benjamin Franklin* ..	12	130
VI. *Appreciations of Light*	18	69
VII. *Relation of Light to Sickness and Health*	13	51
VIII. *Phototropism and Adaptations of Life to Light*	4	7
IX. *Unclassified*	71	124

This analysis revealed that school children of Grades 1 to 6 have some background of knowledge and experience relative to light. It revealed that this background concerns not only electricity, life, mechanical motion, radio activity, chemical action, and heat as manifestations of energy, but also the heavenly bodies, phototropisms, and adaptations of life to light, the relation of light to health, and the nature, manifestations, and properties of light. Since the analysis also revealed that there were more statements from the children concerning the Light–Life phase, it furnished an additional objective basis for the definite selection of this phase for study.

The information, obtained from the statements of these children relative to the energy objective as restricted to the Light–Life phase of the transformation of energy, was utilized in constructing the tests which were used with the experimental teaching classes and for guidance in the presentation and gradation of the instructional content.

CHAPTER V

A Preliminary Discussion of Differences in Learning on Lower and Higher Grade Levels

As THIS is a study of the application of a principle of science teaching which concerns unification, gradation, and sequence of content from kindergarten to university, the question of differentiation of learning on lower and higher grade levels is of paramount significance.

Freeman,[1] when discussing this point in connection with a criticism of proposals to use the objective type of aim as a means to unification, sequence, and gradation, suggests the lack of experimental data on the question as follows: "How may the stages in the development toward the broad generalizations be marked off? What difference in treatment is involved from that which has been used in elementary school science? . . . The question is, namely, what is the difference in the intellectual outlook and the intellectual power of children at different ages, and how does this difference affect instruction in science?"

Contrasts in learning on higher and lower grade levels are presented in detail later in connection with the data from the teaching experiment,[2] but the statements from which the analysis in Chapter IV resulted, though they are preliminary and meager quantitatively, yield some information.

Two blocks of these children's statements pertinent to the objective of the study (Green plants convert the energy of light into the energy of food and fuel) will be presented in detail as a basis for discussion. These two blocks are Energy, Section I A, (General, Unclassified) and Energy, Section I C (The Light–Life Phase).[3]

---

[1] *Thirty-First Yearbook of the National Society for the Study of Education*, Part I, pp. 345-353, 1932. A Program for Teaching Science.

[2] See pages 82-100 of this study.

[3] See pages 25-27 of this text.

SECTION I A
GENERAL. UNCLASSIFIED
Eleven Elements. Frequency of 69

Statement	Grades						
	1	2	3	4	5	6	7
Light is a source of energy.				1	2	1	2
Light is very powerful.			1	1		1	
Power if lit will make light.						1	
Light is used for many purposes.			1	1	3	2	
Light is very precious to man.			1		3	2	
Light is very useful to nature.			1		1	3	
We have to pay for light.	1	1	2				
We should make good use of light.						1	
Light works factories and runs in many towns.						1	
Light is very useful for running electric motors and dynamos, etc.							1
Light is very useful.	1	9		10	5	5	4

SECTION I C
RELATION OF LIGHT TO PLANT GROWTH AND METABOLISM
Eight Statements. Frequency of 91

Statement	1	2	3	4	5	6	7
Without sunlight we would have no flowers or green plants.	1		6	11	9	13	12
Plants grow in sunlight.			2	2	3	8	14
Light gives plants food.					1	1	1
Light is needed in the manufacture of oxygen by plants, trees, and flowers.						1	2
When plants make food with light it is called photosynthesis.				1			
Electric light is not good enough to make plants grow.							1
The sunlight gives color to flowers, etc.						1	
Flowers get yellow when there is no sunlight.							1

SECTION I C
PRODUCTS OF PLANT GROWTH AND METABOLISM MAKE HEAT AND LIGHT
Twenty-two Statements. Frequency of 379

Statement	1	2	3	4	5	6	7
Wood gives light.	1	2	6	35	39	18	9
Light comes from oil.	1	4	3	31	30	20	22
Light comes from gas.	1	1	4	23	26	27	20
You take fire and the little piece of glass which you fasten on the fire. Then you put glass over the part that makes the light.		1					

PRODUCTS OF PLANT GROWTH AND METABOLISM MAKE HEAT AND LIGHT (*Continued*)

Statement	1	2	3	4	5	6	7
Gas must have light.		1					
Gasoline.			1		3		
We use coal for the engine.				1			
Wick.				1			
You get gas light from the air.				1			
Kerosene burns.				1		1	
Gasoline burns.				1		1	
Sterno.					1		
Peat.					1		
Some kinds of oil burn.						1	1
Gasoline lamps.						1	
Alcohol will burn very easily causing light						1	
Wood gives a higher flame because the size is bigger.						1	
Kerosene gives light.				1	15	2	5
Coal gives light.				1	7	1	
Oil comes from vegetables.					1		1
Gas comes from oil.							1
Coal has to burn to give gas.							1

SECTION I C

EFFECT OF PRODUCTS OF PLANT GROWTH AND METABOLISM ON ANIMAL METABOLISM

Nine Statements. Frequency of 104

Statement	1	2	3	4	5	6	7
We could not live without sunlight (*Perhaps* there was awareness of the plant as intermediary).	3	2	7	4	10	13	13
All of us need light (*Perhaps* there was awareness of the plant as intermediary).		2					
If it were not for light we could not live for we could not get food. And therefore we could not live.			3	2	5	2	7
We would not have meat to eat.			1				
If there were no sunlight there would be no plants or animals or people on the earth.					2	3	7
We and animals need light and heat in order to live.					3	4	1
Without light plants and animals could not live, therefore man could not live. ..					2		3
We need plants for the food they make.					1		3
Next to heat and food, light is the most important thing in the world.							1

SECTION I C

ANIMAL METABOLISM PRODUCES LIGHT

Six Statements.   Frequency of 29

Statement	Grades						
	1	2	3	4	5	6	7
Fireflies give light.	1			5	9	5	1
Deep sea fishes give light from their eyes.				1	1	1	
Fireflies give off light in the dark.					2		
Fireflies cause light when it flies by friction of its wings flapping.						1	
Besides fireflies there are other insects which give light, though not to us. However, I think it very unlucky for them because birds and other creatures that eat them can see where they are.						1	1
There is still another kind of light—it is cold light—a light that is not produced by heat or fire—its origin is not known.							

SECTION I C

PRODUCTS OF ANIMAL METABOLISM PRODUCE LIGHT

Nine Statements.   Frequency of 168

Statement	1	2	3	4	5	6	7
A candle gives light.	5	8	12	17	40	18	32
Before we had electricity we had the whale oil lamp.			1	3	2	1	5
The first light was a piece of fat with a wick.			2	1		1	2
Candles are made of tallow.				1			
It is the burning wick of the candle which makes the light.				1		2	
The wax and string give the light of the candle.					1	2	4
Light comes from some fishes that come from the depths of the sea.						1	1
The Indians used a candle fish for light.							3
Some oils that make light come from animals.							2

SECTION I C

LIGHT PRODUCES ANIMAL GROWTH

One Statement.   Frequency of 11

Statement	1	2	3	4	5	6	7
Light helps us to grow.	1			2	1		7

Not all of these statements are directly pertinent to the objective chosen for study—Green plants convert the energy of light into the energy of food and fuel—and not all of them convey their meaning clearly. But if the statements which do satisfy these conditions are grouped by grades, some differences between those made on lower and higher levels become apparent. (The statements from the first, third, and sixth grade levels will be thus grouped. If the same statement was made on the first, third, and sixth grade levels, it is recorded below for the first grade level only; if on both the third and the sixth, it is recorded for only the third.)

Statements Pertinent to the Objective from the First Grades

Wood gives light.
Light comes from oil.
Light comes from gas.
Fireflies give light.
A candle gives light.
Light helps us to grow.
Without sunlight we would have no flowers or green plants (made but once).
We could not live without sunlight (doubtful if there was knowledge of the rôle of the green plant as intermediary).

Statements Pertinent to the Objective from the Third Grades

Plants grow in sunlight.
Without sunlight we would have no flowers or green plants.
Light is used for many purposes.
Light is very powerful.
Light is very precious to man.
Light is very useful to nature.
If it were not for light we could not live for we could not get food. And therefore we could not live.
We would not have meat to eat.

Statements Pertinent to the Objective from the Sixth Grades

Light is a source of energy.
Light works factories and runs in many towns.
Light gives plant food.
Light is needed in the manufacture of oxygen by plants, trees, and flowers.
The sunlight gives color to flowers, etc.
Some kinds of oil burn.
Coal gives light.
If there were no sunlight there would be no plants or animals or people on the earth.

We and animals need light and heat in order to live.
It is the burning wick of the candle which gives the light.
The wax and the string give the light of the candle.

What characteristics differentiate the statements made on the lower grade levels from those made on the higher grade levels?

It is apparent that the statements are statements of association between the concept *light* and one or more other concepts. Thus the statement "Wood gives light" is one of relationship between the concepts *light* and *wood*. "Plants grow in sunlight" is one of relationship between the concepts *plants, growth,* and *sunlight,* and "Light is a source of energy" is a statement of relationship between the concepts *light* and *energy*.

The differences between the statements made on the lower and higher grade levels are differences in concepts and in the association of concepts.[4] The differences may be defined as follows.

I. *The concepts needed for the associations made on the lower grade levels depend upon few experiences which are easily given or acquired.* Thus, the concept *candle* can be easily presented to children; they are familiar with the concept *light* (as the phenomenon needed in this association); and the statement of association "A candle gives light" is a relatively simple one.

II. *The concepts needed for the associations made on the higher grade levels depend upon series of experiences which must be related and held. These experiences are not so easily acquired or presented.* The sixth grade statement "Light is a source of energy" is illustrative. While the concept *light* (phenomenon) may be familiar to very young children, acquisition of the concept *energy* requires the presentation of a series of experiences which must be related and held. Thus this statement is a more complex one than "A candle gives light" and in the learning process would follow acquisition of the latter element.

III. *More concepts are associated in the statements made on the higher grade levels.* This difference is not so strikingly illustrated in the few statements that are presented as it is in the more voluminous data given later,[5] but evidences of this difference are here apparent.

It must be kept in mind that this preliminary presentation of the differences in learning on lower and higher grade levels is based

[4] See pages 82-87, where these differences are discussed in relation to the children's generalizations.
[5] See pages 52-79.

upon statements pertinent to the objective which were obtained *prior* to any controlled instruction. But the same differences appear here as appear more distinctly and consistently in the post-instructional test data.

The descriptions of the teaching procedures for the various grade levels[6] demonstrate how such differences, as indicated above, affected the instruction given on ascending grade levels. Briefly, it may be said here that while every idea presented to the children on all of the six grade levels was contributory to an understanding of the objective, the children of the lower grade levels lost interest more quickly than the children on higher grade levels in (1) ideas which expressed relationships between many concepts and (2) ideas associating concepts which required for their acquisition a considerable range of experience.

[6] See pages 42-51. These descriptions give an answer to the question which was mentioned on page 28—What shall be the difference in *practice* on successive grade levels? The post-instructional data give evidence of the difference in *learning* on lower and higher grade levels when the same objective is used.

CHAPTER VI

Experimental Testing Throughout the First Six Grades of an Elementary School

ALTHOUGH the objective toward which the instruction was to be directed had now been clearly defined and some content contributory to the objective had been determined, instruction of the experimental classes of the Horace Mann Elementary School could not yet begin. Some of the pre-instructional knowledge which was held by these children concerning the material to be presented needed to be determined.

This information was sought for two purposes:

A. Guidance and adjustment in instruction.

B. Comparison with the statements made after instruction for information concerning

1. The effect of instruction on the ideas held before instruction.

2. The effectiveness of the instruction in imparting ideas which were not held before instruction.

This pre-instructional information was first sought from the children of Grades 4, 5, and 6 by using three tests. The first test follows.

Boys and Girls of the Horace Mann School:

Below is a list* of sentences which tell you things about plants. Some of these you will be sure of, some you will be doubtful of, and some you may know nothing about or think wrong. After carefully reading the statements, put an *S* in front of those you are sure of, a *D* in front of those you are doubtful of, an *X* in front of those you know nothing about, and a *W* in front of those you think wrong.

There is a space left below each statement in which you may write anything you might want about any of them.

1. (Green) Plants grow in the sunlight.

2. (Green) Plants make food with (in the presence of) light.

* The statements of this list are reproduced in the words in which they were given by the children and the authorities (pages 22 and 25-27). In certain cases, words are inserted in parentheses in order to make the statements correct.

3. Light is needed by green plants to make oxygen.
4. Without sunlight we would have no green plants.
5.† Light gives plants food.
6.† Electric light is not good enough to make plants grow.
7.† The sunlight gives color to flowers.
8.† Flowers get yellow when there is no sunlight.
9. Plants must have light to live.
10. Sunlight is the power that is used in the plant factory.
11. Plants grow toward the light.
12. The green plant is the only living thing in the world that can make food.
13. Chlorophyll in some way changes sunlight into useful chemical energy.
14. Green plants can make food in sunlight from carbon dioxide and water.
15. The green color due to chlorophyll needs light in which there takes place a chemical process.
16. The (green) plant has a factory in which air, water, and sunlight are turned into food for the plant to grow.
17. Whenever the rays of the sun fall upon the (green) plant leaf the plant takes in carbon dioxide from the air and builds it up into the chemicals of life.
18. Some plants, such as mushrooms, can live in the dark but only when they get food that has been stored up by green plants which grew in the sunlight.
19. Light is needed by (green) plants to make the starch.
20. A potato can grow in the dark but it uses food that has already been stored up.
21. (Green) Plants in the dark die after awhile from lack of food.
22. Deep in the water the plant life does not have a green color which shows that little, if any, light reaches it.
23. During the night green plants cannot make food except with artificial light.
24.‡ Food making by plants can take place only in sunlight.
25. Plants with green leaves must have light to grow.
26. Violet and red lights are useful and green lights useless to help (green) plants use the carbon dioxide properly.
27. Vitamin A is formed by the action of sunlight on green leaves and is not found much in plants grown in the dark.
28. The plant changes energy of sunlight into energy of chemical combination.
29. When plants make food with light (the process) is called photosynthesis.

The foregoing test was constructed from statements which were secured from the analysis of the source treatises concerning light (Light–Life phase, page 22) and from the analysis of the children's responses concerning light (Light–Life phase, pages 25-27). Except as indicated, the first eight statements were

† No attempt has been made to rectify this statement.
‡ This incorrect statement was intentionally inserted.

taken from the analysis of the children's papers and the remaining twenty-one from the analysis of the source treatises.

After the results from this test were examined, it was believed that the test was inadequate. Accordingly, two different additional tests were used. The first of these additional tests, given one week later, consisted of having the children write all they could concerning the "Effect of Light on Plants" or "The Relation of Light to Plants." These topics were written on the blackboard and oral instructions to "write about the topics" were given.

The third week the following additional test was given:

Boys and Girls of the Horace Mann School:

We want you to tell us all you can about the relation of light to plant life. Here is a list of words that will give you ideas. Write your sentences so as to use as many of these words as you can. You may use the words as many times as you like.

Air	Artificial Light	Carbon Dioxide
Water	Vitamin	Photosynthesis
Sugar	Oxygen	Chlorophyll
Starch	Green Color	Chemical Process
Aquarium	Red Light	Plants That Are
Green Leaf	Violet Light	White or Yellow
Factory	Making Food	Electric Light
Hydrogen		

From the analysis of these three tests the pre-instructional test data for Grades 4, 5, and 6 were assembled. In the assembling of these data little weight was given to the results from the first test. For example, consider the following case:

On the first test a child indicates that he knows that "chlorophyll changes sunlight into useful chemical energy." In his essay "The Relation of Light to Plants" no intimation of such knowledge is given and when presented in the third test with suggestions like "green color," "chlorophyll," and "chemical process," no pertinent responses are made. In such a case the knowledge concerned was not credited as being possessed by the child, but statements were retained which appeared in the second test and not in the third, or in the third test and not in the second. In such cases of retention it must be kept in mind that many of the statements were vaguely correct or wholly incorrect.

Children of Grades 1, 2, and 3 cannot express themselves in writing, or do so very inadequately. So the children of these grades were questioned orally and individually, being guided by the following general plan of questioning:

1. We would like to find out what you boys and girls know about flowers and plants. I will ask you some questions. Will you answer them as well as you are able?

2. Why do you put plants near the window? (The replies to this, as to all questions, led to further questioning which varied for each pupil. The questioning in this, as in all cases which follow, was continued until the child could no longer reply with other than "I don't know.")

3. Why do plants bend toward the light?

4. (Attention was directed to a shoot of corn which has been growing so that the lower 4 inches of the plant have been shaded. By questioning, attention is directed to the difference in color.) Why is one part yellow and the other part green?

5. (Plants are shown in a fish bowl.) Why are plants put in a fish bowl? Are they of any use? To the fish? To the water? Are the fish of any use to the plant?

6. What do plants need in order to live? Why do plants need these things? What does the plant do with them?

7. Can plants grow in electric light? (Reasons for answer are asked for.)

8. Where do we get our food? Where does the plant get its food? Could we live without plants? Why?

The records of the pre-instructional and post-instructional conversations with an average second grade child are given below.

Virginia T. Second Grade   C. A. 7-10.   I. Q. 116.   M. A. 9-11

Before Instruction

Q. Do you know what a plant is?
A. Yes. Over there are some. (Pointing to some potted plants on a shelf near the window.)
Q. Do you have any plants at home?
A. Yes.
Q. Who takes care of them?
A. I do.
Q. Where do you keep them? Where do you keep them in the daytime?
A. I put them in the sun.
Q. Why?
A. To grow.
Q. How does the sun make them grow?
A. They need light to live.
Q. Do the plants need anything else besides light?
A. They need water.
Q. Anything else?
A. No answer.
Q. Could you put the plants in electric light to grow?

A. No.

Q. Why not?

A. Because it isn't hot enough.

Q. You see this plant growing here. Why is one part green and this other part (shaded) yellow?

A. I don't know.

Q. Do you notice any special way these plants are growing? (Plants showing heliotropism.)

A. They are all growing toward the window. Why is that?

Q. Well, why is it?

A. Because they are different flowers.

Q. What do you mean by that?

A. The leaves turn.

Q. Why do the leaves turn? What do you mean?

A. No reply after several attempts to obtain one.

Q. In our bowl of fish we have plants. Why?

A. For the fish to have food.

Q. Anything else?

A. Shakes head in negative.

Q. Do the plants help the fish in any way?

A. No reply. Seems uninterested.

Q. Do the plants help the water in any way?

A. No interest. No reply.

Q. Could the water or fish help the plant in any way?

A. The water makes the plant grow. It is a water plant.

Q. What does a plant need in order to live?

A. Plants need air.

Q. Anything else?

A. They need water.

Q. Anything else?

A. Not that I know of.

Q. Where do we get the food we need in order to live?

A. I don't know. (Shows no interest.)

Q. Where do plants get food?

A. I don't know.

Q. A while ago you said that plants needed light to live. Why do they need light?

A. Well, they just have to have it, that's all. Plants can't get along in the dark.

Q. Can't some plants live in the dark?

A. They must have light.

Q. Virginia, you have done very well. Is there anything you would like to tell me about plants which I haven't asked you?

A. I know that you don't have to water cactus plants so often.

· After Instruction

Q. Virginia, we have been talking about plants and flowers and sunlight in class and now I would like to find out what you have learned from these lessons. I will ask you some questions and will you answer them as well as you can?

Q. Why do we put plants near the window?
A. So they will get light.
Q. And why do they need light?
A. So they can grow.
Q. But how does light help them to grow?
A. Light makes them get green. A green plant will grow but a yellow plant will die. And the plants get yellow in the dark.
Q. That is very good. And why will a green plant grow?
A. No answer.
Q. Then perhaps you can tell why a yellow plant will die.
A. No answer.
Q. Do plants need anything else besides light?
A. They need water, soil, sun, and air.
Q. Why do they need these things?
A. To live.
Q. How do these help the plant to live?
A. Plants get their food from the water, soil, sun, and air.
Q. How?
A. Well, these things are the food.
Q. But these things are not food for us.
A. No, but plants can get their food from these.
Q. And where do we get our food?
A. We get our food from the farms. We get it from plants. We could not live without plants.
Q. What would happen to this (indicating a potted green plant) if we should place it in the darkness?
A. It would get yellow.
Q. Anything else?
A. It would die.
Q. Why would it get yellow?
A. Because plants get green in the light.
Q. Do you know of other reasons why it would get yellow in the dark?
A. It would just get yellow. That's all I know.
Q. Why would the plant die in the dark?
A. Well, it would get yellow and wilt and die.
Q. Could we put the plant in electric light and keep it from getting yellow and dying?
A. Electric light is not as good as sunlight for the plant because sunlight has more power.
Q. What do you mean by that? Why does the sunlight have more power?
A. Because it does. That's all I can tell you. You know how strong sunlight is. Why it is the strongest thing in the world.
Q. Can you tell me why these plants are kept in the fish bowl with the fish?
A. Because the plants take air out of the water.
Q. Can you explain some more about this?
A. No. That's all I know about it.

Q. Virginia, you have answered very well. Better than you did the first time you told me about plants. Is there anything else now you might want to tell me?

A. I guess I have told you about all I know about it.

During the pre-instructional and post-instructional conversations, four persons were in the room: the child, the questioner, and two students from the department of Natural Sciences of Teachers College who recorded the procedure verbatim. The presence and activities of these auditors were kept as inconspicuous as possible.

For determination of the post-instructional knowledge in the first three grades, the pre-instructional testing program was again used. In the fourth, fifth, and sixth grades, only the last two of the pre-instructional series of tests were used.

CHAPTER VII

Teaching for Interpretations in Terms of an Objective

IN THE first three grades the lessons were twenty minutes in duration and were given once a week. In Grades 4, 5, and 6 the lessons were thirty minutes in duration and were given once a week. There were five lessons for first grades, six for second and third, nine for fourth, four[1] for fifth, and ten for sixth grades.

DATA CONCERNING THE CHILDREN

First Grades. *Total Number 32*

Median I.Q.	121.5	Range in I.Q.	91–140
Median C.A.	6–6	Range in C.A.	5–11—7–10
Median M.A.	7–11	Range in M.A.	5–7—10

Second Grades. *Total Number 40*

Median I.Q.	·116.5	Range in I.Q.	87–142
Median C.A.	7–7	Range in C.A.	6–7—9–3
Median M.A.	9–0	Range in M.A.	6–11—10–6

Third Grades. *Total Number 22*

Median I.Q.	119	Range in I.Q.	100–140
Median C.A.	8–6	Range in C.A.	7–7—9–3
Median M.A.	9–9	Range in M.A.	8–11—11–11

Fourth Grades. *Total Number 37*

Median I.Q.	115	Range in I.Q.	95–144
Median C.A.	9–6	Range in C.A.	8–7—10–5
Median M.A.	11–5	Range in M.A.	9–8—13–11

Fifth Grade. *Total Number 17*

Median I.Q.	109	Range in I.Q.	96–127
Median C.A.	10–8	Range in C.A.	9–11—12–2
Median M.A.	11–8	Range in M.A.	10–2—13–3

Sixth Grades. *Total Number 21*

Median I.Q.	118	Range in I.Q.	96–165
Median C.A.	11–4	Range in C.A.	9–9—13–6
Median M.A.	13–8	Range in M.A.	11–1—17–10

[1] Because of unforeseen changes in the school schedule the number of lessons in the fifth grade was reduced. The presentation was therefore inadequate.

The purpose of the teaching was to approach an interpretation of certain learning experiences in terms of the objective "Green plants convert the energy of light into the energy of food and fuel."

The following observations and experiments were used as an approach on all six of the grade levels.

A potted plant and a large crayon-colored picture of a green plant were used to show the main parts of a plant: root, stem, leaf, and flower. Experiments were then done by teacher and pupil to show that green plants turn toward the light; that green plants get yellow in the dark; that such yellow plants then become green again if placed in the light; and that green plants finally die if left for long in the dark.

Beyond this introductory presentation the instruction which was given on each of the six grade levels differed.

The First Grades

An attempt at interpretation of the phenomena presented in terms of energy transfer was not satisfactory. Perhaps the closest approach to instruction was in connection with the development of the idea that animals get their food from green plants, directly or indirectly. The following diagram was developed with the children and seemed to be appreciated by them:

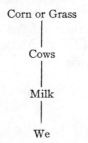

Corn or Grass

|

Cows

|

Milk

|

We

The idea that plants "need" water, soil, sun, air, and food was developed, but no direct attempt was made to teach the distinction between "food" and "water, air, and soil."

The teacher stated several times that food is made by the green plant in the presence of sunlight.

The children knew that if you put green plants in an aquarium with fishes you do not usually have to change the water so often; but the nearest approach to an explanation which seemed possible[2] was that the plants "give out good air for the fishes to breathe in."

Illustrative Material Used. Potted green plant. Crayon-colored drawing of a green plant showing root, stem, leaf, and flower. Balanced aquarium. Film, "Sunshine," 16mm., National Carbon Company, Cleveland, Ohio.

Experiments and Demonstrations. *Teacher*—Putting green plant near window to show turning toward the light. *Pupil*— Putting green plant in the dark to observe color change. Sprouting two potatoes, one in the dark and one in the light, to observe difference in color.

The Second Grades

An attempt at the desired interpretation of the phenomena met with more success with the second grade than with the first grade children. It was possible to make some reference to energy (strength or power) resulting from the sun and sunlight. The opportunity arose when the children inquired concerning the moving vanes of a radiometer which had been placed near a window. The radiometer was taken to a shaded part of the room and the children saw the motion of the vanes cease. They were then told that it was the light "force," or power from the sun which caused the motion and that when sunlight falls upon a green leaf this power from the sun is stored by the green leaf as food strength. The idea that animals get their food, directly or indirectly, from green plants then developed. The following are schemes which were presented by the children:

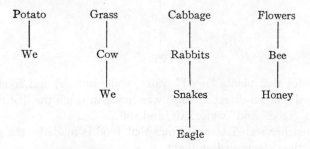

Potato	Grass	Cabbage	Flowers
We	Cow	Rabbits	Bee
	We	Snakes	Honey
		Eagle	

<hr />

[2] See pages 82-87 for information concerning bases for judging the possibility of presenting an idea on any grade level.

The idea also developed that certain plants like fungi (toadstools and mushrooms) depend upon green plants for food. The children were told that since such plants were not green they could not make food.

Some progress seemed to have been made in presenting distinctions between "food" and "water, air, and soil." For example, it seemed clear that we could live on "food" but that we could not live on "air, water, and soil."

The children knew that if you put green plants in an aquarium with fishes you do not usually have to change the water so often but little progress was made toward a correct scientific explanation.

Illustrative Material Used. Potted green plant. Large colored drawing of a green plant. Balanced aquarium. Film, "Sunshine," 16mm., National Carbon Company, Cleveland, Ohio.

Experiments and Demonstrations. Teacher—Putting green plants near window to show turning toward the light. Placing radiometer in direct and diffused sunlight. *Pupil*—Putting green plant in the dark to observe color change.

Third Grades

After the general preliminary presentation of phenomena of the relation of light to plant life, the approach to interpretation through the use of the radiometer, as described for the second grades, was attempted.

The children were told that when sunlight falls upon a green leaf the energy (strength) of the sun, which caused the motion of the radiometer vanes, is in a sense stored in the plant as food. An attempt was made to explain how our strength comes from green plants and thus is, in the final analysis, from the light of the sun. The following diagrams were discussed by the children:

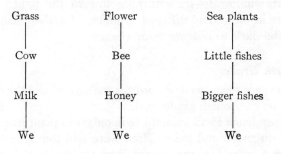

Grass	Flower	Sea plants
Cow	Bee	Little fishes
Milk	Honey	Bigger fishes
We	We	We

The children were told that light energy causes plants to turn toward the window, because in this position more light energy falls upon the leaf and thus more energy is stored in food; that green plants die in the dark because all of the manufactured food has been used and, of course, no more can be made in the absence of light.

An attempt to interpret the phenomena of color change seemed unsuccessful. This may have been due to the fact that the children did not seem interested in the cross-section of a green leaf, chlorophyll bodies, stomata, etc.

An attempt was made to explain why plants need water and air as well as light. These children did not seem interested in discussions of oxygen, nitrogen, and carbon dioxide, but they did seem to understand something of the distinction between a "food" and "air, water, and soil." The following lists of substances which are and are not foods were constructed by them:

Not Foods	Foods
Ground	Meat
Air	Potatoes
Stones	Lettuce
Iron	Bread
	Milk

There was reference to the fact that the green plant received more energy from the sun than from electric light, but no attempt at explanation was made.

Illustrative Material Used. Potted green plant. Large colored drawing of a green plant. Balanced aquarium. Film, "Sunshine," 16mm., National Carbon Company, Cleveland, Ohio.

Experiments and Demonstrations. Teacher—Putting green plant near window to show turning toward the light. Placing radiometer in direct and diffused sunlight. *Pupil*—Putting green plant in the dark to observe color change.

The Fourth Grades

The same approach, as described for the second and third grades, was used on the fourth grade level.

The dependence of all animal life upon green plant life for food had been discussed and the children were told that when sunlight falls upon a green leaf the energy from the sun, which made the radiometer move, is utilized by the green plant in food making. It was explained that green plants turn toward the window in response to light and in this position receive more energy for food making; that green plants die in the dark because all of the food which has been made has been used and no more can be made without light.

An interpretation of the phenomena of color change seemed to meet with some success. The children showed interest in a slide under a microscope showing a cross-section of a lilac leaf and in a large colored blackboard drawing of the microscopical appearance of this slide. The drawing was called "A View of Nature's Food Factory." It remained on the board for several weeks and formed the basis and focus of reference for discussions. The following parts were labelled: Upper Skin, Palisade Cells, Chlorophyll bodies (The Food Machines), Spongy Layer, Vein, Stomata or Air Holes, and Lower Skin.

The children spoke of water as being a composition of oxygen and hydrogen and of air as containing carbon dioxide and oxygen. A food (starch) was said to be composed of carbon, hydrogen, and oxygen.

The following description of a food came from the class:

A food should
1. Give strength
2. Make you live
3. Make blood.

"Oxygen gas" and "carbon dioxide gas" were used in discussions of the relations of fishes, green plants, water and sunlight as found in the balanced aquarium. The following diagram was discussed:

Green Plant

There was some discussion of the spectrum of sunlight and electric light. Sunlight was passed through a prism and the children saw the emergent band of colors. They were told that the energy available for food making differed for various parts of the spectrum. They were also told that the spectrum from ordinary electric light was not the same as that from sunlight.

The following diagram was discussed:

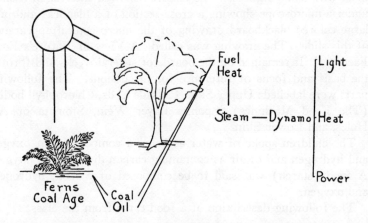

Illustrative Material Used. Potted green plant. Large colored drawing of a green plant. Balanced aquarium. Film, "Sunshine," 16mm., National Carbon Company, Cleveland, Ohio. Film, "Energy from Sunlight," 16mm., Eastman Educational Films. Large blackboard drawing of cross-section of a green leaf. Cross-section of a lilac leaf through a compound microscope. Blackboard chart showing Oxygen–Carbon Dioxide Cycle. Blackboard chart showing energy transformations from sun to heat, light and power.

Experiments and Demonstrations. Teacher—Putting green plant near window to show turning toward the light. Placing radiometer in direct and diffused sunlight. Placing prism in sunlight. *Pupil*—Putting green plant in the dark to observe color change and ultimate death.

The Fifth Grade

See note at the bottom of page 42.

The approach used for the second and third grades was also used on the fifth grade level.

The following scheme developed from the discussion with the children:

Likeness of a Green Leaf to a Factory

Power	Raw Materials	Product
Sunlight	Air	Starches, sugars, and oils
	Water	(food)
	Ingredients of soil	

These children spoke frequently of the energy of coal and food as derived from sunlight. They were told that green plants turn toward the window because in this position light energy for food making is available; that green plants die in the dark because the stored food has been used and no more can be made in the dark.

There was little explanation of color change given. Neither microscopic slide nor blackboard drawing of the cross-section of a green leaf was used, as was done in the fourth grade instruction. The children were simply told that the leaf contains little bodies in which the food is made; that the green color of the leaf is due to these bodies; and that these green bodies become inactive and tend to become colorless in the dark.

Oxygen and hydrogen were used when speaking of the composition of water, and carbon dioxide and oxygen when speaking of the parts of air. A food was referred to as a combination of carbon, oxygen, hydrogen, and sometimes nitrogen.

There was only casual reference to the interrelations of fishes and green plants in an aquarium.

There was no direct instruction pertaining to the comparative effects of sunlight and artificial light upon green plants.

Illustrative Material Used. Potted green plant. Large colored drawing of a green plant. Balanced aquarium. Film, "Sunshine," 16mm., National Carbon Company, Cleveland, Ohio. Film, "Energy from Sunlight," 16mm., Eastman Educational Films.

Experiments and Demonstrations. Teacher—Putting green plant near window to show turning toward the light. Placing radiometer in direct and diffused sunlight. *Pupil*—Putting green plant in the dark to observe color change and ultimate death.

The Sixth Grades

The approach used for the second and third grades was also used on the sixth grade level.

The dependence of all animal life upon green plants for food was discussed and it was explained to the children that all of the energy for plant and animal life and motion is derived, through the green plant, from the sun.

There was discussion of the gases composing air and water and the utilization of carbon, oxygen, and hydrogen in food making.

The children learned that green plants turn toward the window so that they can receive as much light energy as possible for food making; that green plants die in the dark because all of the food has been used and no more can be made in darkness.

It was possible to make some interpretation of the phenomena of color change. A slide showing the cross-section of a lilac leaf was viewed through the compound microscope and a large colored drawing of the appearance of this slide was placed on the blackboard. The drawing was entitled "A View of Nature's Food Factory." It remained on the blackboard for several weeks and formed the basis and focus of reference for discussions. The following parts were labelled: Upper Skin, Palisade Cells, Chlorophyll Bodies (The Food Machines), Spongy Layer, Vein, Stomata or Air Holes. The action of these different parts of the green leaf in the presence and absence of light was discussed.

A green leaf was compared to a factory. The following scheme developed:

Comparison of Green Leaf and a Factory

Power	Light
Machinery	Chlorophyll bodies
Materials	Carbon dioxide and water (H_2O)
Product	Starches and sugars
Storerooms	Cells in the plant
Waste product	Oxygen

The spectrum of sunlight and the electric light were compared. Sunlight was passed through a prism and the children saw the emergent band of colors. They were told that the available energy for food making differed for different parts of the spectrum. They were also told that the same spectrum does not result from electric light as from sunlight.

There was mention of the fact that ordinary window glass filters out some of the spectrum of the sunlight.

The relation between green plants, fishes, and sunlight in the balanced aquarium was discussed. There was development of the idea that when green plants are in the presence of light they make food from carbon dioxide and hydrogen taken from the water; that in this process of food making oxygen, which fishes must breathe in, is given out by the plant and that the carbon dioxide used by the green plant comes from material exhaled by the fish. This process of exchanges of gases between green plants and animals in the presence of light was explained as taking place, not only in water, but wherever green plants, animals, and light are associated. Upon the suggestion of several children breath was blown into lime water to show that the milky precipitate is a test for carbon dioxide.

Illustrative Material Used. Potted green plant. Large colored drawing of a green plant. Balanced aquarium. Film, "Sunshine," 16mm., Eastman Educational Films. Blackboard drawing of a cross-section of a green leaf. Slide of cross-section of a green leaf observed through a compound microscope.

Experiments and Demonstrations. · *Teacher*—Putting green plant near window to show turning toward the light. Placing radiometer in direct and diffused sunlight. Placing prism in the sunlight. Breathing into lime water. *Pupil*—Putting green plant in the dark to observe color change and ultimate death. Breathing into lime water.

SPECIAL DIFFICULTIES WHICH INFLUENCED THE COURSE AND DURATION OF INSTRUCTION

The following are special difficulties that were encountered and that influenced the course and duration of instruction:

The explanation of "food" as a combination of various elements (not so difficult in Grades 4, 5, and 6 as in the first three grades).

Explanation of air and water as composed of various elements (not so difficult in Grades 4, 5, and 6 as in the first three grades).

Presentation of idea of cross-section of a green leaf (especially difficult only on the first three grade levels).

Distinction between respiration in green plants and the process of photosynthesis.

CHAPTER VIII

The Test Data

IN THE organization and treatment of the test data the following plan is used:

I. The pre-instructional and post-instructional data are presented by grades.

II. For each grade level the data are organized by the following units:

A. Necessities for Plant Growth and Life (exclusive of mention of Food and Fuel Making).

B. Effect of Light on Plants (exclusive of mention of Food and Fuel Making).

C. Interrelations of Plants and Animals (exclusive of mention of Oxygen and Carbon Dioxide Cycle).

D. Relation of Light to Animal Life (exclusive of mention of Plants as Intermediaries).

E. Comparison of Natural and Artificial Lights and Their Effects upon Plant Life.

F. Food and Fuel Making by Plants. Where the Plant Gets Food.

G. Oxygen and Carbon Dioxide Cycle. The Balanced Aquarium.

III. For each grade level tables are presented showing for each unit:

A. The number of different statements which were made before and after the instruction.

B. The number of these statements which were correct.

C. The number which were incompletely correct, equivocal, or vague.

D. The number which were entirely wrong.[1]

IV. The children's pre-instructional and post-instructional state-

---

[1] These children's statements are organized under the three classifications "correct," "vague," and "wrong" in data which are on file in the Teachers College library.

ments are given by units for each grade level. Each statement is followed by a number which indicates the percentage of the class which made that statement. Thus, the statement from the first grade data "Plants must have light to live" (47) means that 47 per cent, or 15 pupils, of the class of 32 pupils made that statement.

V. For each grade there is presented an analysis of the entire data for that grade level relative to the attainment of the objective of instruction. Some statements are presented at this place which may not have been classified under any of the seven units.

FIRST GRADES

Thirty-Two Pupils

BEFORE INSTRUCTION

	No. of Statements	Correct	Vague	Wrong
Unit A	6	1	5	0
B	12	1	5	6
C	0	0	0	0
D	0	0	0	0
E	2	0	1	1
F	2	1	1	0
G	3	0	2	1
Total	25	3	14	8

AFTER INSTRUCTION

	No. of Statements	Correct	Vague	Wrong
Unit A	7	0	7	0
B	10	0	9	1
C	4	1	3	0
D	0	0	0	0
E	0	0	0	0
F	11	0	5	6
G	12	0	6	6
Total	44	1	30	13

COMPOSITE FIRST GRADE CONCEPTION

UNIT A

Before Instruction

Plants must have light to live (47). Plants need air to grow (34). Plants need water (13). Plants with green leaves must have light to grow (3). Plants need dirt (3). Plants need fresh air (3).

After Instruction

Plants need water, sunshine, soil, and air (72). Plants need water, soil, and light (25). Plants use water, sunshine, soil, and air to live (9). Plants need water, food, and fertilizer (3). Plants need water and sun (3). Plants need water, air, and sun (3). Plants need water so they wont die (3).

UNIT B

Before Instruction

Plants grow in the sunlight (47). Plants grow toward the light (28). Without sunlight we would have no green plants (25). Plants get yellow when there is no sunlight (22). The sunlight gives color to plants (3). Plants get yellow because they don't get air (3). The plant gets yellow because there is water (3). Plants grow better in the sun but dark is almost as good (3).

Plants bend over to the window because they don't get air and water (13). Wind makes plants bend toward the window (6). Plants bend toward the window because they will die (3). Plants bend to the window because they are heavy (3).

After Instruction

Plants get green in the light (81). Plants get yellow in the dark (53). A plant turns yellow in the dark and then dies (47). Plants die in the dark (41).

Plants turn to the window to get light because light makes them strong (56). Plants bend to the window to get lots of sunlight (25). Plants bend to the window to get air (9). Plants bend to the window to get light because they must stay green (3). Plants bend to the window to get sun so they will get fatter (3).

Sun makes plants strong (13).

UNIT C

Before Instruction

None.

After Instruction

We get our food from plants (66). We could not live without plants, because animals that we eat live on plants (50). We could not live without plants because we eat plants (13). We get our food from animals and plants (9).

UNIT D

Before Instruction

None.

After Instruction

None.

UNIT E

Before Instruction

Electric light is not good enough to make plants grow (31). Plants would grow with electric light (3).

After Instruction

None.

UNIT F

Before Instruction

When plants are green they are alive (19). Dead plants are yellow (or brown) (16).

After Instruction

Plants make food (9). Plants make food—they get some water and soil (3). Plants make food with sun and water (3). Plants are the only things that can make food (3).

A green plant is the strongest kind of a plant (9).

Plants get their food from the ground or dirt (35). Plants get their food from people (12). Plants get their food from the ground, water, and air (9). Plants get their food from water, soil, and sun (9). Plants get their food from the roots (6). Plants get their food from the air (3).

UNIT G

Before Instruction

Plants are in an aquarium to give food to fishes (6). If you put plants in an aquarium you don't have to change the water (3). Plants are in a fish bowl because plants like to have them around (3).

After Instruction

Plants keep the water in the fish bowl healthy for the fish, you would have to change the water often if it were not for plants (3). Green plants make the water healthy (3). Plants keep the water in the fish bowl fresh. They put something in the water (3).

Plants keep the water in the fish bowl clean (6). The plant cleans the fish bowl (3). The plant sucks up the dirt in the fish bowl (3).

Fishes eat the plants in the fish bowl (59).

We could not live without plants because we take the oxygen into our lungs and turn it into another kind of oxygen which the plant takes in. Plants give out oxygen and we take that in. Oxygen is in the air, you could not breathe without it (3). We could not live without plants because they breathe out the stuff we breathe in and we breathe out what they breathe in (3).

Plants make the fish feel more at home (3). Fish like the plants in the fish bowl (3).

The plant eats the water in the fish bowl (3).

FIRST GRADE STATEMENTS EVIDENCING OR IMPLYING ATTAINMENT OF THE OBJECTIVE

There are no direct statements from the children of this grade level pertaining to energy transfer, but the following are worthy of note:

Plants turn to the window to get light because light makes them strong (56). Sun makes plants strong (12).

We could not live without plants because animals that we eat live on plants (50).

SECOND GRADES

Forty Pupils

BEFORE INSTRUCTION

	No. of Statements	Correct	Vague	Wrong
Unit A	5	1	4	0
B	12	1	6	5
C	0	0	0	0
D	0	0	0	0
E	2	0	1	1
F	2	1	1	0
G	9	0	4	5
Total	30	3	16	11

AFTER INSTRUCTION

Unit A	5	0	5	0
B	6	0	4	2
C	5	0	5	0
D	0	0	0	0
E	12	10	1	1
F	26	2	16	8
G	17	0	10	7
Total	71	12	41	18

COMPOSITE SECOND GRADE CONCEPTION

UNIT A

Before Instruction

Plants must have light to live (55). Plants need water (25). Plants need air (13). Plants need soil (13). Plants need food (3).

After Instruction

Plants need water, air, soil, and light (55). Plants need water, soil, and light (38). Plants need air, sun, and water (8). A plant dies in the dark (5). Plants need water, soil, and food (3).

UNIT B

Before Instruction

Sunlight makes plants grow (73).

Without sunlight we would have no green plants (13). Plants get yellow when there is no sunlight (10). Plants get green in the light (5). Air and sunlight make plants yellow (3). Plants get yellow in the dark because of water (3). Water makes the leaf green (3). Sap makes the plant green (3).

Plants grow toward the light (10). Plants grow toward the window because of weight (3). Plants make plants bend toward the light (3). Plants bend toward the window to get fresh air (3).

After Instruction

Plants turn to the window to get light (95). The stem bends plants to the window (3).

Light makes plants green (63). A plant gets yellow and dies in the dark (60). Plants get yellow in the dark (28). A plant in the dark gets dirty air and then gets yellow (3).

UNIT C

Before Instruction
None.

After Instruction

Our food comes from plants (93). We could not live without plants (43). We could not live without plants because we eat plants for food (20). The animals that we eat get their food from plants (15). Our food comes from light (3).

UNIT D

Before Instruction
None.

After Instruction
None.

UNIT E

Before Instruction

Electric light is not good enough to make plants grow (33). Electric light is not as good as sunlight to make plants grow because it is not as hot (28).

After Instruction

Electric light is not as good as sunlight to make plants grow (69). Electric light is not as good as sunlight because sunlight has more power (47). Electric light is not as good as sunlight because sunlight is warmer (33). Electric light is not as good as sunlight for plants because it is not as bright (15). Electric light is not as good as sunlight because it has not the same rays (6). Sunlight is better for plants than electric light (6). Sunlight is best for plants (6). Sunlight does more than electric light (3). Electric light is not as strong as sunlight and so the plant cannot make food with it (3). Sunlight is better for plants than light because sunlight has food in it (3).

Both electric light and sunlight help plants grow (9).

An arc light is as good for plants as sunlight (3).

UNIT F

Before Instruction

Dead plants are yellow (or brown) (15). Live plants are green (8).

After Instruction

Plants make food from sun, air, water, and soil (10). Plants make food with the help of sunlight (3). A plant makes food (3). Plants make food with soil and water (3). Plants make food from air, sun, and water (3).

The plant mixes sun, soil, and water and makes food (5).

The green plant is the kind that makes food (3). Some plants can't make food (3). The green in a plant helps it to grow (3).

Green plants are the best and healthiest (8).

When you put bulbs in the dark they take food that has been stored up and then get yellow (8). Plants get yellow and die in the dark because they have no light to make food (3). Plants will grow for a couple of days in the dark (3).

Plants store food in the root (8). Plants store the water, soil, and sun as food (3).

Plants get their food from the ground (38). Plants get their food from water, soil, and light (20). Plants get their food from the stem (8). Plants get their food from the roots (5). Plants get their food from the soil and the water that is in the soil (5). Plants get their food from soil and sunshine (3). Plants get food from light (3). Plants get food from fertilizer (3). A plant would die in the dark because the sunshine is part of the food (3).

We can't make food like plants can (5).

Mushrooms get food from trees (3).

UNIT G

Before Instruction

Plants are put in the fish bowl to give the fish food (20). There is something in plants the fishes like (5). Plants are put in the fish bowl to give the fish insects (3).

Plants draw up something from the water (3). Plants make the water fresh (3). Plants clean the aquarium by sucking up everything (3). Plants keep the water healthy (3). Plants get dirt from the water (3).

Plants get dirt from plants (3).

After Instruction

Fishes give out bad air and the plants take this in and give out good air (5). Fish breathe in oxygen and the plant gives them oxygen to breathe in (3). Fish breathe out carbon dioxide and give it to the plants (3). If you take the plant out of the fish bowl the fish would use up all of the air in the bowl (3). Fish get fresh air from the plants in a fish bowl. Fish breathe out dirty air and plants give them clean air (3). Plants take air out of the water (3).

Plants clean the water in the fish bowl (23). Plants clean the fish bowl by sucking up the dirt in the water (5). Plants keep the water in the fish bowl clean so you don't have to change the water every day (3). In a fish bowl dirty water goes into the plant and clean water comes out of it (3).

We could not live without plants because they give out good air (3). We could not live without plants because they breathe in carbon dioxide and give out oxygen (3).

Plants breathe in bad air and breathe out good air (3). Plants breathe in bad air (3).

Carbon dioxide which we give out is bad air—oxygen is a good air (3).

The plants are put in the fish bowl to give the fish food (43). Plants give food to the water in the fish bowl (8).

SECOND GRADE STATEMENTS EVIDENCING OR IMPLYING ATTAINMENT OF THE OBJECTIVE

There are no direct statements from the second grade group after instruction pertaining to the transfer of energy and there are no statements which seem to approach the conception as closely as the three mentioned for the first grades.

THIRD GRADES
Twenty-Two Pupils
BEFORE INSTRUCTION

	No. of Statements	Correct	Vague	Wrong
Unit A	4	1	3	0
B	12	1	7	4
C	0	0	0	0
D	0	0	0	0
E	2	0	2	0
F	2	0	0	2
G	16	0	7	9
Total	36	2	19	15

Unit A	4	0	4	0
B	7	0	7	0
C	5	1	3	1
D	1	0	1	0
E	7	0	7	0
F	19	1	8	10
G	12	0	11	1
Total	55	2	41	12

COMPOSITE THIRD GRADE CONCEPTION

UNIT A

Before Instruction

Plants need light (68), water (64), and soil (23).
Plants need air to breathe (32).

After Instruction

Plants need soil, water, sunshine, and air (91). Plants need sunshine, air, and soil (5). Plants need water and sunshine (5). Plants need water, soil, and light (5).

UNIT B

Before Instruction

Sunlight helps plants to grow (86). Plants get yellow when there is no sunlight (82), when there is no air (5), when there is water (5), when there is heat (5). Plants grow toward the light (77). Plants with green leaves must have light in order to grow (50).

Sap (5), water and earth (5), rain (5), and air and oxygen (5) make plants green.

Air pushes the plant to grow toward the window (14).

After Instruction

Plants bend toward the window to get light (86) . . . so they won't get yellow for they won't live long in the dark (5). Plants get yellow and die in the dark (82). Plants get green in the light (77). Green plants in the dark lose the food and turn yellow (9). In the dark the plant would lose all of the food in it and then get yellow and die (9). Plants get yellow in the dark (5).

UNIT C

Before Instruction
None.

After Instruction
We could not live without plants for they give animals and us food (100?). We get our food from plants (73).
All animals get their food from plants (32).
Plants get their food from us (5).
We could not live without plants (18).

UNIT D

Before Instruction
None.

After Instruction
The sun makes us grow (5).

UNIT E

Before Instruction
Electric light is not good enough to make plants grow (77) . . . because it does not give off as much heat (5).

After Instruction
Electric light is not as good as sunlight because it is not as strong (36), it does not have the power (32), sunlight has more rays and colors (5), the same things are not in electric light (5), it is not as warm (5), it is artificial (5).
Electric light is not as good as sunlight for plants (9).

UNIT F

Before Instruction
Plants get food from dirt (5), rain (5).

After Instruction
The green plant makes food (27) . . . from water, soil, sunshine, and air (18) . . . from sunshine (5), from water and sun (5). A plant gets yellow and dies in the dark because it cannot get sunlight and so it cannot make food for itself (13).

Plants put water, sun, soil, and air together to make food (5) which is put in the root and then pushed from the root up into the plant (5).

Plants get their food from the ground (23) . . . from air, water, light, and soil (9) . . . from roots (9) . . . soil and sun (5) . . . water and soil (5) . . . air (5) . . . sun (5) . . . water and sun (5).

Plants eat sunshine, rain, and soil (5).

A green plant grows better (9).

Bulbs store food (9).

We can't make our own food (5).

UNIT G

Before Instruction

Plants are put in the fish bowl so that fish can eat them (32) . . . to give air to fishes (13) . . . to take air out of the water (5) . . . to purify the water (5) . . . to give out breath to the water (5) . . . to take poison out of the water (5).

Fish breathe out carbon which the plants breathe in (5). Plants breathe out oxygen which the fish breathe in (5). Plants' breath is dry and good for the fish, fishes' breath is damp and good for the plants (5). The plant takes the kind of air out of water that people can't breathe (5). The plant puts the kind of air into the water that people breathe (5). Air goes into the plant from the fish (5).

Plants do something for fish (5). Plants keep the fish bowl clean (5). Fish like plants around (5). The carbon keeps the plant alive (5).

After Instruction

Plants are put in a fish bowl to give the fish food (50).

Plants put clean air in the fish bowl (32). They take bad air (poisonous air) out of the water and put good air into the water (9). They keep the water in the fish bowl fresh (5). They put something in the water which cleans it (5). Fish breathe out bad air and the plant gives the fish good air (5). Plants give the fish air (9). Plants have to do with air and oxygen (5). The plant lets out good air for the fish—you breathe good air in and let out bad air. The fish lets out bad air and the plant purifies the air (5). What we breathe out the plant gets and makes into fresh air (5).

Plants keep the fish bowl clean (5). If you put plants in the fish bowl you do not have to change the water (5).

The first two of the following statements are contained in the preceding unit organization. The last two statements were not classified under any of these units:

Electric light is not as good as sunlight because it is not as strong (36). Electric light is not as good as sunlight because it does not have the power (31).

The power from sunlight goes into the plant (4). When we eat plants we are eating sunshine (4).

FOURTH GRADES
Thirty-Seven Pupils

BEFORE INSTRUCTION

	No. of Statements	Correct	Vague	Wrong
Unit A	7	3	4	0
B	5	0	5	0
C	1	0	1	0
D	0	0	0	0
E	3	0	3	0
F	12	3	5	4
G	3	0	3	0
Total	31	6	21	4

AFTER INSTRUCTION

	No. of Statements	Correct	Vague	Wrong
Unit A	10	1	9	0
B	5	0	5	0
C	3	1	2	0
D	6	0	6	0
E	5	1	3	1
F	45	6	29	10
G	14	0	8	6
Total	88	9	62	17

COMPOSITE FOURTH GRADE CONCEPTION

UNIT A

Before Instruction

Plants must have light (73) . . . water (73) . . . air (35)

. . . soil (19) . . . oxygen (3). Plants need light, air, and oxygen (3).

Plants with green leaves must have light to grow (16).

After Instruction

Sun and light help plants to grow (70). Plants need water (32) . . . air (32) . . . soil (22) . . . oxygen (3). Plants need air, water, and light to live (3). Plants need water, air, and soil to live (3).

Carbon dioxide, oxygen, and hydrogen make the plant grow with sunlight (5).

Plants must have light but sunlight is best (5).

A plant cannot live in the dark (65).

UNIT B

Before Instruction

Light helps plants to grow (97). Sunlight makes the leaf green (46). Plants grow toward the light (16). Plants get yellow when there is no sunlight (5). Water makes the plants get green (5).

After Instruction

Light makes leaves green (59). Leaves get yellow in the dark (43).

Plants turn toward the sun (54) . . . because the sun has such strong rays in it (3).

Sunlight makes plants strong (3).

UNIT C

Before Instruction

There is a kind of plant that eats flies (3).

After Instruction

If we did not have sunlight we could not live because we eat animals and they eat plants (32). We could not live without plant food (8). We get our food from the plant (8).

UNIT D

Before Instruction

None.

After Instruction

The sun helps us to grow (8) . . . makes us well (8) . . . makes us brown (8) . . . keeps us alive (5) . . . gives strength to people (3) . . . gives us heat (3).

UNIT E

Before Instruction

Electric light is not good enough to make plants grow (32).
Artificial light will help plants grow (3).
Plants will grow in red light (3).

After Instruction

Plants will not grow as well in electric light as in sunlight (5). It will help plants if they cannot get sunlight (3). Electric light does not make plants grow (3).

Two of the colors of sunlight we cannot see with our eyes, they are ultra-violet and infra-red (3). Sunlight has many colors in it (3).

UNIT F

Before Instruction

Plants make food with light (16). Some plants, like mushrooms, can live in the dark (11). The plant has a factory in which air, water, and sunlight are turned into food for the plant to grow (3). The plant is the only living thing in the world that can make food (3). Light is needed by plants to make starch (3). Food-making by plants can take place only in sunlight (3). During the night the green plants cannot make food except with artificial light (3).

Light gives plants food (14). The plant eats dirt (14). The plant gets nourishment from the soil for the plant to make food (3). Plants get nourishment from water (3).

Dead plants are brown (3).

After Instruction

The sun makes the leaf factories go (46) . . . which makes food (19) . . . starch (5). If you put a plant in the dark it will not have green in its leaves because the little machines that make food for the plant stop working (32). Plants make the food (30) . . . sugar (14) . . . which helps them to grow.

The plant uses the energy of sunlight to make sugar out of carbon dioxide and oxygen that is in the air and hydrogen that is in the water (14). The plant will make food with water, soil, and other things (5). Plants make sugar and starch (5). The little air holes in the plant take air and the veins bring the water up to the little cells which are machines in a plant and the green leaves take in the sun and with these the little cells in the plant make food (3). Plants cannot live without sunlight because out of particles of light the plant can make food (3). The leaf is the most important part of the plant for making food (3). Air gives oxygen and hydrogen for plants to make food out of, and also nitrogen (3). Plants make food (3) . . . sugar (3) . . . out of air and water. The leaves of the plant make nearly all of the food for it is the leaves of the plant that take in air and light and have the green color (3).

A plant cannot live without sunlight because light makes the little cells in the plant work like a machine and this gathers water, soil, and air and with these things it makes its food (14). Sunlight and air help make food for the plant to grow on (3). Plants make food out of air and water (3).

Plants get oxygen from both air and water and so they have some oxygen to give out (8). Plants take in oxygen and carbon dioxide but they only take the oxygen (5).

Some plants can live in the dark (8). A bulb may grow in the dark until its food is used up (5). A potato growing in the dark uses food that has already been stored up (3). A plant in the dark will not grow because the leaves turn yellow (3). In the dark the little green cells of the plant will not run (3). The green plant will die without sun (3).

There are plants that are not green, like toadstools (8). Mushrooms and toadstools are white, they cannot make food (3). Every plant that is not green gets its food from a green plant (3). Some plants cannot make their own food, so they grow on other plants—the mushroom is one of these, it grows on trees and takes the strength from the trees (14). Plants will turn yellow or white if they get no light because chlorophyll, the thing that makes plants green, comes from the sun (3).

Sunlight gives plants food (16). The sun makes food (8). If the plant has no light it takes food from the root or other part of the plant (3). The roots of a plant get the food but some of the food comes from the leaves (3). Plants must have air because it gets most of its food from the air (3). Plants breathe air and that makes food (3).

Plants must have food (3).

No man can make food (8).

Every plant has factories (5). It is the ultra-violet in the sun that works the machines (3).

Green plants make coal (11). The sun makes coal (8).

Water gives oxygen to the plant (3).

UNIT G

Before Instruction

Plants must breathe oxygen just as we do (3). Plants breathe with oxygen (3). Plants breathe the air that we breathe out (3).

After Instruction

Plants in a fish bowl give out oxygen (16). Fish breathe out carbon dioxide and plants breathe in carbon dioxide (11). The plant breathes out oxygen and the fish breathes in oxygen (11). Plants breathe in carbon dioxide and breathe out oxygen (8). Plants take in carbon dioxide from the breath of the fish (5). Fish breathe out oxygen and breathe in carbon dioxide (5).

If you put a plant in a fish bowl, both the fish and the plant will grow and you don't have to change the water. This is because the plant gives out oxygen and takes in carbon dioxide (5). Plants that live in the water get air out of the water (3). We breathe out oxygen and breathe in carbon dioxide (3).

Fish could not live without a green plant (5). In a fish bowl the plant keeps the fish alive and the fish keep the plant alive (3). Plants keep fish alive (3).

Plants in a fish bowl clean the bowl (3). In a fish bowl there are plants to eat up the dirt and give the fish food (3).

FOURTH GRADE STATEMENTS EVIDENCING OR IMPLYING ATTAINMENT OF THE OBJECTIVE

Some of the following statements have already been classified under the unit arrangement of data for this grade level:

If we did not have sunlight we could not live because we eat animals and they eat plants (32).

Light gives energy to plants (18). Sun makes the energy in green plants ('16). Light gives strength to the plant (13). Sunlight makes life in plants (5). The leaves of a plant get the energy from the sun (2). Sunlight makes plants strong (2). When you eat vegetables you are getting some of the energy from the sun which the plant has stored up (2). Light gives energy to plants to grow (2). The sun gives power to plants (2).

Some plants cannot make their own food, so they grow on other plants. The mushroom is one of these, it grows on trees and takes the strength from the trees (13).

We get strength from green plants (18).

The sun makes electricity (8). The sun makes wind and the wind makes windmills go (2). Light will turn an instrument called a radiometer (2).

Wood and power are from a plant and we make machines run with that (5).

The sun gives strength to people (2).

Electricity makes trains go (2).

FIFTH GRADE
Seventeen Pupils
BEFORE INSTRUCTION

	No. of Statements	Correct	Vague	Wrong
Unit A	4	2	2	0
B	5	0	4	1
C	0	0	0	0
D	0	0	0	0
E	3	0	2	1
F	12	0	10	2
G	4	0	3	1
Total	28	2	21	5

AFTER INSTRUCTION

	No. of Statements	Correct	Vague	Wrong
Unit A	3	0	3	0
B	3	0	3	0
C	2	1	1	0
D	0	0	0	0
E	0	0	0	0
F	17	3	13	1
G	5	1	3	1
Total	30	5	23	2

COMPOSITE FIFTH GRADE CONCEPTION

UNIT A

Before Instruction

Plants must have light to live (88) . . . water (41) . . . air (29). Plants with green leaves must have light to grow (6).

After Instruction

Plants could not live without sunlight (24). Plants need sunlight, water, and soil (6). Some plants need oxygen to grow (6).

UNIT B

Before Instruction

Sunlight makes plants grow (71) . . . makes plants green (18). Plants get yellow when there is no sunlight (12). Plants grow toward the light (6). The green plant takes the green color out of the sun (6).

After Instruction

Light makes plants grow (18). The plant follows the sun (12). The sun keeps the plant leaf green (12).

UNIT C

Before Instruction

None.

After Instruction

If we did not have plants we would die because we would have nothing to eat (29). Animals live on plants so we have to have the plants even though we live on animals (18).

UNIT D

Before Instruction

None.

After Instruction

None.

UNIT E

Before Instruction

Sunlight is stronger than electric light (6). Electric light helps plants to grow (6). Electric light kills plants (6).

After Instruction
None.

UNIT F

Before Instruction

Light is needed by plants to make starch (24). The plant makes food with the help of light (24). The plant has a factory in which air, water, and sunlight are turned into food for the plant to grow (24). Plants make sugar which is their food (12). Green plants make food with light (6). Plants make food with sun and water (6) . . . with air and water (6). The plant takes certain elements from the sun which it makes into food (6).

Plants get their food from light (24).

The plant is the only living thing that can make food (6).

Plants make coal (6).

Plants that are white have not as much starch as the green leaf (6).

After Instruction

If you put a plant in the dark it will die because it cannot make food (65). Plants get yellow in the dark because they do not have the sun to give energy to make food (65). Plants make food with the help of light (47). The plant turns yellow because the factories can't make any more food for the plant to grow on (24). Sunlight gives plants the power to mix air and water to make sugar and starch and oil for the plant to grow on (18). The food factory is in the leaf (12). Earth and water are made into sugar, starch, and oil (12). A plant does not use water, air, soil, and sunlight as food but it makes its food from these (6). A plant becomes yellow because the factory has stopped and the plant has used up all the food it has stored (6). White plants cannot make their own food as green plants can (6). The green part of the plant that is in the sun makes food and sends it down to the root which cannot make food (6).

A plant in the dark with plenty of good soil and water would never live unless it had been in the sunlight and had stored up a little food with which it could live for awhile (24).

If you put a plant in electric light the food factories will run but not so well as in sunlight (18).

No person can make food (18).

The potato stores food so it can live better (12).

A mushroom takes the sugar, starch, and oil from the tree upon which it is growing or from decaying green plants (6). A seaweed is green because it is on top of the ocean and when it goes down it gives food to the other plants that are not green on the ocean bed (6).

UNIT G

Before Instruction

Plants breathe air (12). People's air is oxygen (6). Carbon dioxide is the best air for plants (6). The plant changes carbon dioxide into oxygen (6).

After Instruction

Plants give oxygen to the air which is good for us (24). In a balanced aquarium the green plant gives out oxygen which the fish breathes in and the fish breathes out carbon dioxide which the plant takes in and you have just enough plants and fish (12). If you had a fish in the fish bowl and had no plants the fish would die (6). A plant breathes just the same as we do (6). Oxygen and carbon dioxide are quite different. We breathe out carbon dioxide. Plants breathe in both and breathe out oxygen (6).

FIFTH GRADE STATEMENTS EVIDENCING OR IMPLYING
ATTAINMENT OF THE OBJECTIVE

Some of the following statements have already been classified under the unit arrangement of data for this grade level:

Plants get yellow in the dark because they do not have the sun to give energy to make food (65).

Animals live on plants so we have to have the plants even though we live on animals (17). If there were no sun people could not live because the plants take the energy of the sun and give it to us (17).

Sunlight gives plants the power to mix air and water to make sugar and starch and oil for the plant to grow on (17). The plant gets its energy from the sun (17). Light helps plants to make energy (5).

An electric light can give some energy having received it from the sun, the place where most electricity is found (5).

SIXTH GRADES

Thirty-Six Pupils

BEFORE INSTRUCTION

	No. of Statements	Correct	Vague	Wrong
Unit A	6	3	3	0
B	7	1	6	0
C	0	0	0	0
D	1	1	0	0
E	1	0	1	0
F	13	2	8	3
G	3	0	3	0
Total	31	7	21	3

AFTER INSTRUCTION

	No. of Statements	Correct	Vague	Wrong
Unit A	3	1	2	0
B	8	1	5	2
C	8	5	3	0
D	0	0	0	0
E	18	3	7	8
F	39	12	26	1
G	9	1	5	3
Total	85	23	48	14

COMPOSITE SIXTH GRADE CONCEPTION

UNIT A

Before Instruction

Plants must have light to grow (83) . . . water (36) . . . dirt (36) . . . air (31) . . . oxygen (3). Green plants must have light (14).

After Instruction

Plants cannot live without water, air, and light (25) . . . sunlight (19). Plants need water (6).

UNIT B

Before Instruction

Plants grow in sunlight (72). Without sunlight we would have no green plants (42). Light helps plants (31). Leaves get yellow when there is no sunlight (17). Plants grow toward the light (14). The sun opens the leaves (3). Sunlight helps plants to grow (3).

After Instruction

Plants turn white or yellow in the dark (50). The plant will lose all of its chlorophyll without sunlight (47). Plants turn toward the light (25). Sunlight makes plants grow (14). If it were not for light there would be no green plants (11). The sunlight gives leaves their color which is another way of saying that the sun keeps plants alive (3). Plants turn yellow in the closet because they get no air (3). Sunlight has chlorophyll (3).

UNIT C

Before Instruction

None.

After Instruction

Man cannot live without plant life because animals eat plants that make food (39). Without sunlight there would be no vegetation, without vegetation there would be no animals and without sunlight, vegetation, and animals there would be no man on the face of the earth (11). Humans and animals and plants that are white or yellow depend on green plants for their food (8). Plants give us food (8). We could not live without plants (6).

Plants cannot live without animal life and animal life cannot live without plant life (8). The plant cannot live without animal life (6). Fish rot and their bodies make good fertilizer (3).

UNIT D

Before Instruction

We could not live without sunlight (3).

After Instruction

None.

UNIT E

Before Instruction

Electric light is not good enough to make plants grow (47).

After Instruction

The colors in sunlight are red, orange, yellow, green, blue, indigo, and violet (22). The colors in sunlight are as follows: red, orange, yellow, green, blue, and purple (3). The colors in sunlight are as follows: red, orange, yellow, green, blue, white, lavender, and orchid (3). Some of the most important colors of sunlight are: ultra-violet, blue, purple, and green (3).

The violet ray in sunlight is very good for plants (14). Violet light gives the plant power (3). The violet, green, and blue rays of sunlight possess the most energy (3). The purple color of sunlight is most important for plants (3).

Electric light does not do any good for plants because it has not the violet, blue, and green rays (11). Electric light will not make plants grow because it is missing two things, the red light and the violet light, mostly the violet light (11). Electric light is not as good as sunlight for plants (8). The violet, green, and blue in sunlight possess the most energy and electric light has little energy (6). Artificial light is good for plants (3). The different rays of sunlight are: ultra-red, red, orange, yellow, blue, light and dark green, violet, and ultra-violet. The three former give heat and these alone are in electric light (3).

Red, orange, and yellow are heat rays of sunlight (6). Red is one of the colors of sunlight that gives heat (3).

Infra-red and ultra-violet are not visible to the human eye (3). Ultra-violet is not visible to the human eye (3).

UNIT F

Before Instruction

Plants make food with light (28). Sunlight is the power that is used in the plant factory (22). Food making by plants can take place only in sunlight (22). The sun makes the green leaf factory run (13). The plant has a factory in which air, water, and sunlight are turned into food for the plant to grow (11). Plants make food from water and air (8). The plant makes food (3).

Light is needed by green plants to make oxygen (14).

Light gives plants food (11). Sunlight gives plants nourishment through the leaves (6).

Plants could not grow without carbon dioxide (6).

Some plants, such as mushrooms, can live in the dark but only when they get food that has been stored up by green plants which grew in sunlight (19). The green color in leaves is good for plants (3).

After Instruction

The plant makes sugar and starch with the help of sunlight (69). If the plant does not get light it cannot live for it cannot live without chlorophyll for chlorophyll helps make the food (53). The sun gives the leaf the energy to make food (47). If you put a plant in the dark it will turn yellow and die because it cannot make food unless it is green (44). The chlorophyll (green color) in the leaves acts like a machine, and through the energy of the sun makes food which is stored in the stem and leaves of the plant (42). The plant would lose all of its power to make food without sunlight (39). Only green plants can make food (33). Plants make their own food (28). Plants must have water, air, soil, and sunlight to make food (22). Photosynthesis means making food with light (17). If you put a plant in the dark it will die because it cannot make food (14). A plant in comparison with a factory:

Chlorophyll	Machines
Sunlight	Power
Leaves and trunk	Storehouses
Water, carbon dioxide, and fertilizer	Material
Starch and sugar	Product (14)

The food making of plants is called a chemical process (11). If the leaf has everything it needs it will make food (11). A plant is only making food in the light, for it is somewhat like a factory, the light being the power and the chlorophyll the machines (11). Plants cannot make food in the dark but in the dark they use food that has been stored up which they made in the light (8). The materials that the green plant uses to make food are: carbon dioxide, water, and fertility (8). This is how the plant makes food: $CO_2 + H_2O = CHO$. The wasted oxygen goes out the air holes of the leaf (6). Food is made by the energy of sunlight (3).

Nothing else but plants can make food (17).

Chlorophyll is the green color in the leaf (29). The green coloring matter in a leaf is contained in the palisade cells and is called chlorophyll (6). Green color makes plants grow (6).

Coal comes from green plants that grew in the sunlight (19). Peat comes from green plants that grew in the sunlight (6).

Electric light is not so good for plants to make food because it does not have ultra-violet light (14). Sunlight is made of the colors red, orange, yellow, green, blue, indigo, and violet and a red and violet color which we cannot see but which are important to the plant for making food (3). A plant in making food must have violet light and red light (3).

Sugar and starch feed the plant and help to give energy as well (8). The food of the plant is carbohydrate (8). Starch is food for the seeds (3). Sugar and light make starches and other necessary things for the plant (3). Sugar is made of three chemicals (3).

Water contains hydrogen which plants need to make food (3). Air has carbon dioxide and oxygen which plants need to live (3). The plants use air to make food (3). Hydrogen is something which plants put in starches (3).

Light gives us food (3).

Plants are the one power of this world (3).

UNIT G

Before Instruction

Plants breathe air (8). Plants in an aquarium give oxygen to fish (8). Plants make the air pure (3).

After Instruction

If you put a plant in the fish bowl it is good for the fish because in the light plants give out oxygen for the fish to use and the fish give out carbon dioxide just as we do so there is a cycle between the fish and the plant (28). When at night the sun goes away a change comes over the plant. Instead of taking in carbon dioxide and letting out oxygen (opposite from humans) it will breathe in oxygen (14). Human beings breathe in oxygen and breathe out carbon dioxide (8). The grass in an aquarium gives oxygen to fish (6). The plants in the daylight breathe in carbon dioxide and breathe out oxygen and we do the opposite so it keeps on going around but in the night the plants breathe like we do (6). Plants in an aquarium breathe carbon dioxide (3). Plants breathe off air (3). If you put an aquarium of fish in the dark the fish will die because they cannot get air from under the water (3). The plant breaks up carbon dioxide and gives out oxygen (3).

SIXTH GRADE STATEMENTS EVIDENCING OR IMPLYING
ATTAINMENT OF THE OBJECTIVE

Some of the following statements have already been classified under the unit arrangement of the data for this grade level:

Sunlight gives energy to plants (63). The sun gives the leaf the energy to make food (47). The chlorophyll (or green color) in the leaves acts like a machine, and through the energy of the sun makes food which is stored in the stem and leaves of the plant (41). The plant would lose all of its power to make food without sunlight (38). The sun is a source of power (27). Sunlight can be transformed to heat, light, and power (13). Without sunlight there would be no vegetation, without vegetation there would be no animals and without sunlight, vegetation, and animals there would be no man on the face of the earth (11). The energy from the sun may be stored and used (11). All power comes from the sun (11). Violet light gives the plant power (2). Food is made by the energy of sunlight (2). Plants convert light into food energy, a cow eats the plant and the plant is converted into animal energy, we drink the milk from the cow and that is converted into human energy (2). Light $\longrightarrow$ plant = food = energy = motion (2). Light $\longrightarrow$ plants = life (2). Sun + hydrogen + oxygen + carbon dioxide = plants = food = energy which can be changed into power energy, which can be changed into motion energy (2).

Men cannot live without plant life because animals eat plants that make food (38).

The sun and plants help make coal and coal gives us heat (16). The sun makes wood which makes fire (8). Thus, from coal and peat, sunlight is turned into heat which runs machines making power (8). Sun energy can be changed into heat energy through fuel (2). Our electricity is made from the sun by means of water and steam (2).

Sugar and starch feed the plant and help to give energy as well (8).

MISCELLANEOUS

THE FIRST GRADES

Before Instruction
None.

After Instruction
None.

THE SECOND GRADES

Before Instruction
None.

After Instruction

Light makes food get better (3). The good part of the light cannot get to plants unless the window is up (3).

THE THIRD GRADES

Before Instruction

None.

After Instruction

Plants inside a window do not do so well as plants outside (5).

THE FOURTH GRADES

Before Instruction

Plants under the sea are different from those living on earth (9).

After Instruction

The sun is powerful (19). When sunlight goes through a glass it is not as good as before (3). Clouds and storm take away some of the sunlight (3). A Japanese Evergreen is the only green plant that cannot live without sunlight (3).

THE FIFTH GRADE

Before Instruction

None.

After Instruction

Light has a lot of power in it (18). A potato is the stem of a plant. The young potato grows from it when in the dark (6). Electricity and energy are about the same (6).

THE SIXTH GRADES

Before Instruction

None.

After Instruction

Window glass does not let through all of the colors of sunlight. It keeps out the ultra-violet (6). The parts of the plant are: roots, stem, leaves, and flower (6). We do not get half as much sunlight as we ought to on account of clothing, smoke, buildings, and indoor work (3). Sunshine will not shine in ordinary window glass (8).

CHAPTER IX

Discussion of the Test Data

THE discussion of the test data will be presented under the following heads:

  I. Unit Organization by Use of the Objective.

  II. Differences in Complexity of the Units.

  III. Grade Differences in Learning of the Units.

  IV. Correlation between Complexity and Grade Learning.

  V. The Errors of the Units.

  VI. Correlation between Errors, Complexity, and Grade Learning.

  VII. Generalization as a Process of Thought.

I. UNIT ORGANIZATION BY USE OF THE OBJECTIVE

The organization by units is a prominent feature of the data and will form a basis for approach to its interpretation. The units of the study are as follows:

A. Necessities for Plant Growth and Life (exclusive of mention of Food and Fuel Making)

B. Effect of Light on Plants (exclusive of mention of Food and Fuel Making)

C. Interrelations of Plants and Animals (exclusive of mention of Oxygen and Carbon Dioxide Cycle)

D. Relation of Light to Animal Life (exclusive of mention of Plants as Intermediaries)

E. Comparison of Natural and Artificial Lights and Their Effects upon Plant Life

F. Food and Fuel Making by Plants. Where the Plant Gets Food.

G. The Oxygen and Carbon Dioxide Cycle. Balanced Aquarium.

The units of this study are stated topically. Each unit implies an understanding. This understanding is contributory to the integrating objective and is developed through learning experiences. These learning experiences are expressed in the statements which compose the units.

Most organizations of learning elements by units are teacher-made. The units of this study are the outgrowth of the results of instruction. An organization of content on the basis of these units was not considered while the teaching was being done. So far as is known no textbook, syllabus, or course of study organizes and presents the content pertaining to the energy relations of light and plants under the above set of units. Certain topics, such as "The Balanced Aquarium," "Food and Fuel Making by Green Plants," and perhaps several others are listed and taught. But this array of units and organization was not in mind before or during the teaching.

What was held in mind by the teacher in selecting, organizing, and presenting the content was the integrating objective "Energy Relations between Light and Green Plants." The selection and amount of this contributory content which was presented on any particular grade level was determined from the interests and reactions of the children, the advice of classroom teachers and auditors, and the judgment of the science teacher.

Since the set of units under discussion emerged upon analysis of the post-instructional test papers, the organization is in this sense the child's and not the adult's; is psychological and not logical.

Such an organization by units reverses the usual process. It is customary for teachers and curriculum workers to write out a set of units and then see how well they will be learned on various grade levels. Here learning experiences have been selected and presented with no thought of unit organization; with an integrating objective as the guide to selection. And the units have emerged after the instruction.

These units proved to be of great help in working with many elements of learning by blocks which in their sum total present an array of content contributory to an understanding of the integrating objective. And as will be explained,[1] they offer suggestions and means for progressively graded teaching pertaining to the integrating objective. Since each element of learning is an integral part of the understanding of a unit, each unit is an integral part of an understanding of the objective, and in consideration of gradation of subject matter, such units can be treated with less confusion than great numbers of separate elements. The topics of these units may be stated in the form of declarative sentences, as

[1] See pages 82-87.

is done later in this chapter where such statements are called "Key Ideas,"[2] and they then become meanings which associate and indicate a certain array of facts.

II. DIFFERENCES IN COMPLEXITY OF THE UNITS

The units are of varying degrees of complexity. Certain units may be said to be simpler than others because the elements composing the units are simpler.

But why can some learning elements be called simpler than others?

An examination of the elements reveals that some depend for their presentation and acquisition upon either merely a single directed observation or, at the most, a simple experiment involving but one or two observations which need to be related; while others depend for their acquisition upon the interposition of experiments or explanations involving a series of observations and ideas which must be related and held.

Examples of the simpler type of elements are:

Plants get green in the light and yellow in the dark.
Plants grow toward the light.
Plants grow in the light.
Plants need water, air, and light to live. (That plants need air is not so easily demonstrated as are the other two necessities.)
The sun gives us heat.

It is evident that many of the above can be presented and learned through a single directed observation and if any can not be learned by this method, the presentation of the element requires but a simple experiment involving a few observations and ideas to correlate.

Examples of the more complex type of learning element are:

Fish breathe in oxygen and breathe out carbon dioxide.
Green plants give out oxygen in the presence of light.
There is an oxygen and carbon dioxide cycle between the fish and the green plant in the presence of, light.
Green plants make food with the help of light.
Green plants store up energy from the sun.
Sunlight can be transformed to heat, light, and power.

It is evident that the learning of any of the above elements requires the association and correlation of numerous observations and

2 See pages 87-88.

ideas. None of the immediately foregoing elements can be taught or learned from a single observation, as is the case with elements of the first list. To learn or teach that "green plants get yellow in the dark" is much simpler than to learn or teach that "green plants make food with the help of light." An understanding of the latter requires the association of a considerable range of ideas. Children know, or easily learn, the meaning of "green plant" and "yellow plant" and the establishment of the relation between "green plant," "yellow plant" and "light" is easy, depending upon a simple observation. But to learn or teach the meaning of "make food" is not so easy and the establishment of the relation between "green plant," "make food" and "light" does not depend upon one simple observation. (More will be said later concerning the building of meaning into concepts like "make food," etc.; pages 90 ff.)

The relations required in the two foregoing illustrative examples may be schematically presented thus:

Green plant————————————Light   Green plant————————————Light
Yellow plant————————————   Make food————————————

It is thus seen that some elements are simpler than others and that, therefore, some of the units are simpler than other units because they are composed of the simpler elements.

A classification of the units as simple or complex on the basis of the considerations just presented follows:

Simple Units	*Complex Units*
Effect of Light on Plants (exclusive of mention of Food and Fuel Making).	Food and Fuel Making by Plants. Where the Plant Gets Food.
Necessities for Plant Growth and Life (exclusive of mention of Food and Fuel Making).	Oxygen and Carbon Dioxide Cycle. The Balanced Aquarium.
Relation of Light to Animal Life (exclusive of mention of Plants as Intermediaries).	Comparison of Natural and Artificial Lights and Their Effects upon Plant Life.
Interrelations of Plants and Animals (exclusive of mention of Oxygen and Carbon Dioxide Cycle).	

As further evidence of the validity of the foregoing basis for classification of elements of learning and units as simple or complex, the relations of the concepts involved in the correct elements of the various units are schematically arranged.

THE SIMPLE UNITS

Effect of Light on Plants
(Exclusive of mention of Food and Fuel Making)

Plants Green ——————— Light	Plants Turn to ——————— Light
Plants Yellow ——————— Dark	Plants Strong ——————— Light
Plants Die ——————— Dark	Plants Grow ——————— Light
Plants Lose chlorophyll ——————— Dark	*Green plant Yellow ——————— Dark Lose food

Necessities for Plant Growth and Life
(Exclusive of mention of Food and Fuel Making)

Plants—Water—Sunshine—Soil—Air——————For life

Relation of Light to Animal Life
(Exclusive of mention of Plants as Intermediaries)

We Get brown ——————— Sunlight	We Alive ——————— Sunlight
We Grow ——————— Sunlight	We Get strength ——————— Sunlight
We Get well ——————— Sunlight	We Get heat ——————— Sunlight

Interrelations of Plants and Animals
(Exclusive of mention of Oxygen and Carbon Dioxide Cycle)

Our food
|
From plants

Sunlight
|
Plants (green)
|
Animals
|
Mankind

* The set of relations involved in this element, found in two cases on the third grade level, is rather complex.

THE COMPLEX UNITS

Food and Fuel Making by Plants
Where the Plant Gets Food

Green plant——
Make food —————————Sunlight

Plant
|
Make food

Plant——
Get yellow————————————Dark
Not make food—

Plant——
Make sugar——
Oxygen   Hydrogen—— Energy of
| | Sunlight
Air   Water—

Plant——
Get yellow———
Die———————————————Dark
Not make food—

Green plant——
Make starch or sugar——Sunlight

Air holes of leaf
|
Air
Veins ——————————
| Light
Water
Machines in green leaf
Make food—————

Plant———————— Dark
Get yellow———
Not make food— No energy

Plant——
Die———
No chlorophyll—————Dark
|
Help make food

Yellow plant——
Not make sugar,
starch and oil———— Light
|
Decaying green plant

Plants——
Not make food———Electric light
No ultra-violet—

Plants——
Not make food————
Use stored food—————Dark

Plants
|
Air from water

Fish
|
Breathe in oxygen

Given out by plant (green)

Fish
|
Breathe out carbon dioxide

To plants

Plants
|
Give out oxygen

Plants
|
Give out oxygen
|
To us

Plants
Give out oxygen ————————— Light
To fish
|
  Give out carbon dioxide

Comparison of Natural and Artificial Lights
and Their Effects upon Plant Life

Electric light
Not so good for plant ————————— Difference in power (or energy)
Sunlight

Electric light
Not so good for plants ————————— More rays and colors
Sunlight

Sunlight
|
Violet light
|
Good for plants

Violet light
|
Power to plants

This diagrammatic arrangement of the elements of learning brings into relief the factors which make for simplicity or complexity of the elements and thus the units which they compose.

In the case of the elements of the simpler units it is seen that few concepts need to be related and held and that the few experiences necessary for the formation of the concepts are easily given. In the case of the elements of the more complex units, however, several or many concepts must be related and held and the experiences necessary for the formation of the concepts are numerous and not so easily presented and acquired.

The learning which took place on the lower grade levels of this study, though elementary, was worth while in itself and at the same time it was contributory to a major objective which served as a selective and integrating device. Thus it is believed that the operation of a rational method of gradation of content has been demonstrated.

III. GRADE DIFFERENCES IN LEARNING OF THE UNITS

In each of the six grades certain units give evidence of having been learned by a majority of the group while other units were not so learned.

It is well to give an idea of what is meant by "learned" and by "majority of the group."

It will be noted that the statements composing each particular unit center about a key idea for that unit. When, then, it is stated that a unit has been "learned," it is meant that this key idea has been expressed by a majority of the group.

UNITS	KEY IDEA
Food and Fuel Making by Plants. Where the Plant Gets Food.	Green plants make food in the presence of light.
Effect of Light on Plants (exclusive of mention of Food and Fuel Making).	Plants become green in the light and yellow in the dark and
	Green plants turn toward light.
Necessities for Plant Growth and Life (exclusive of mention of Food and Fuel Making).	Plants need water, air, light and soil.
Oxygen and Carbon Dioxide Cycle. The Balanced Aquarium.	Green plants in the presence of light give out oxygen and take in carbon dioxide. Fish breathe in oxygen and breathe out carbon dioxide. Thus, in the light, there is a cycle between the fish and the green plant.

Interrelations of Plants and Animals (exclusive of mention of Oxygen and Carbon Dioxide Cycle).

We get our food from green plants.

Relation of Light to Animal Life (exclusive of mention of Plants as Intermediaries).

The sun helps us to grow
or
The sun makes us well
or
The sun makes us brown
or
The sun gives us heat.

Comparison of Natural and Artificial Lights and Their Effects upon Plant Life.

Electric light is not as good as sunlight for the growth of the green plant because it lacks certain of the spectral colors of sunlight.

By "a majority of the group" is meant, approximately, half or more of the group. The nature of the tests used and the manner of recording the data make it difficult to say exactly when half of the group have responded with a given idea. For example, in the fifth grade it was found that eleven of the group said concerning the food making unit, "A plant gets yellow in the dark because it does not have the sun to give energy to make food," and that four said, "The plant turns yellow because the factories can't make any more food for the plant to grow on." It cannot be concluded from this that exactly fifteen of the group made statements concerning food making, for some of those who responded with the latter statement may also have made the former statement.

But knowing the total number of children comprising each group and the total number of children for that group responding to each element, a rather accurate quantitative approximation can be made.

The units successfully and unsuccessfully learned follow:

FIRST GRADES

Learned by Majority of Group

Effect of Light on Plants (exclusive of mention of Food and Fuel Making).

Necessities for Plant Growth and Life (exclusive of mention of Food and Fuel Making).

Interrelations of Plants and Animals (exclusive of Oxygen and Carbon Dioxide Cycle).

Not Learned by Majority of Group

Food and Fuel Making by Plants. Where the Plant Gets Food.

Oxygen and Carbon Dioxide Cycle. The Balanced Aquarium.

Relation of Light to Animal Life (exclusive of mention of Plants as Intermediaries).

Comparison of Natural and Artificial Light and Their Effects upon Plant Life.

SECOND GRADES

Effect of Light on Plants (exclusive of mention of Food and Fuel Making).

Interrelations of Plants and Animals (exclusive of Oxygen and Carbon Dioxide Cycle).

Necessities for Plant Growth and Life (exclusive of mention of Food and Fuel Making).

Food and Fuel Making by Plants. Where the Plant Gets Food.

Oxygen and Carbon Dioxide Cycle. The Balanced Aquarium.

Comparison of Natural and Artificial Lights and Their Effects upon Plant Life.

Relation of Light to Animal Life (exclusive of mention of Plants as Intermediaries).

THIRD GRADES

Necessities for Plant Growth and Life (exclusive of Food and Fuel Making).

Effect of Light on Plants (exclusive of mention of Food and Fuel Making).

Interrelations of Plants and Animals (exclusive of mention of Oxygen and Carbon Dioxide Cycle).

Food and Fuel Making by Plants. Where the Plant Gets Food.

Oxygen and Carbon Dioxide Cycle. The Balanced Aquarium.

Comparison of Natural and Artificial Lights and Their Effects upon Plant Life.

Relation of Light to Animal Life (exclusive of mention of Plants as Intermediaries).

FOURTH GRADES

Necessities for Plant Growth and Life (exclusive of mention of Food and Fuel Making).

Food and Fuel Making by Plants. Where the Plant Gets Food.

Effect of Light on Plants (exclusive of mention of Food and Fuel Making).

Interrelations of Plants and Animals (exclusive of mention of Oxygen and Carbon Dioxide Cycle).

Oxygen and Carbon Dioxide Cycle. The Balanced Aquarium.

Relation of Light to Animal Life (exclusive of mention of Plants as Intermediaries).

Comparison of Natural and Artificial Lights and Their Effects upon Plant Life.

FIFTH GRADE

Food and Fuel Making by Plants. Where the Plant Gets Food.

Oxygen and Carbon Dioxide Cycle. The Balanced Aquarium.

Interrelations of Plants and Animals (exclusive of mention of Oxygen and Carbon Dioxide Cycle).

Necessities for Plant Growth and Life (exclusive of mention of Food and Fuel Making).

Effect of Light on Plants (exclusive of mention of Food and Fuel Making).

Relations of Light to Animal Life (exclusive of mention of Plants as Intermediaries).

Comparison of Natural and Artificial Lights and Their Effects upon Plant Life.

SIXTH GRADES

Food and Fuel Making by Plants. Where the Plant Gets Food.

Effect of Light on Plants (exclusive of mention of Food and Fuel Making).

Interrelations of Plants and Animals (exclusive of mention of Oxygen and Carbon Dioxide Cycle.)

Comparison of Natural and Artificial Lights and Their Effects upon Plant Life.

Oxygen and Carbon Dioxide Cycle. The Balanced Aquarium.

Necessities for Plant Growth and Life (exclusive of mention of Food and Fuel Making).

Relation of Light to Animal Life (exclusive of mention of Plants as Intermediaries).

From the foregoing tables it will be observed that *one unit which was not learned by a majority on the lower grade levels was so learned on higher grade levels.*

Comprehension of the unit "Food and Fuel Making by Plants" is not adequately evidenced (according to the criteria) on the first, second, and third grade levels but is so evidenced on the fourth, fifth, and sixth grade levels. Some observations made during the process of teaching are in place here to help explain this comprehension solely on higher grade levels.

First of all, on the first, second, and third grade levels it was extremely difficult, if not impossible, to approach a scientific explanation of the concept *food*. The interest and reaction of the children indicated that the instruction pertaining to the concept was not effective. The attempt to present the idea of food as a combination of certain elements was more successful on the higher grade levels, but the children of the lower grade levels could not be made to think of food in this way. And very likely an important reason why no progress could be made with the food concept on the lower grade levels was the failure to impart a second fundamental idea—the composition of air and water.

The children of the lower grade levels thought of air and water as homogeneous substances, and very little progress could be made in the instruction toward giving the conception of chemical mixture or combination of gases. It is obvious that a scientific conception of food is dependent upon a scientific conception of air and water. Here, then, is an illustration of the dependence of understanding of an idea or a concept upon the prior understanding of other ideas or concepts.

A third possible reason for lack of comprehension of the food making unit on the lower grade levels may have been the difficulty of presenting the conception of the structure of a green leaf. The children of Grades 4, 5, and 6 were interested in examining slides of a cross-section of a green leaf through a microscope, but the children of the lower grade levels showed little interest in these slides or in the drawings and charts which were successfully used on the higher grade levels.

Also, it will be observed that *certain units which give evidence of having been learned by a majority on the lower grade levels are evidently not so learned on higher grade levels.*

There are three units which show an effect contrary to what would at first thought be expected. The unit "Necessities for Plant Growth and Life (exclusive of Food and Fuel Making)" has been learned by a majority on the first, second, third, and fourth grade levels but not on the fifth and sixth grade levels. The unit "Interrelations of Plants and Animals (exclusive of Oxygen and Carbon Dioxide Cycle)" has been learned by a majority on the first, second, and third grade levels but not on the fourth, fifth, and sixth grade levels. And the unit "Effect of Light on Plants (exclusive of Food and Fuel Making)" shows a decrease in learning toward the higher grade levels.

Now these three units are composed of comparatively simple elements (e.g., "Plants get green in the light." "Plants need air, water, and sun." "Animals depend upon green plants for food."), and since they were learned on the lowest grade levels a continuing increase in learning on higher grade levels might be expected.

It is suggested that these simpler elements and units were learned on the higher grade levels but their acquisition is not revealed. The following explanation is advanced.

It will be noted that it is on those higher grade levels where these simpler units are evidently not learned that the acquisition of the more complex units emerges. For example, evidenced acquisition of the comparatively simple unit "Necessities for Plant Growth and Life (exclusive of Food and Fuel Making)" dwindles on the fourth, fifth, and sixth grade levels, but it is on these same grade levels that learning of the more complex unit "Food and Fuel Making by Plants" emerges. It is therefore suggested that when children of the higher grade levels were presented in the tests with the concept stimuli, for example, *air* or *water* they responded with a more complex statement, such as "Green plants make food with air and water," rather than with a simpler statement, such as "Plants need air and water to live." They responded with the more complex statements because, knowing them as well as the simpler ones, they sensed the relative significance of the more advanced idea.

However, it seems reasonable to believe that had the tests used with the higher levels been made of sufficient length and searchingly minute, acquisition of the elements of the simpler units would have been revealed. (But such tests would have unnecessarily fatigued the children. The acquisition of more complex elements on higher grade levels and the dependence for understanding of complex elements on the acquisition of simpler ones is demonstrated and such determination was one of the chief purposes of the testing.)

Finally, it is observed that *three units were not learned by a majority of any of the groups.* These three units were:

1. Oxygen and Carbon Dioxide Cycle. The Balanced Aquarium.

2. Relation of Light to Animal Life (exclusive of mention of Plants as Intermediaries).

3. Comparison of Natural and Artificial Light and Their Effects upon Plant Life.

There are some considerations pertaining to these units which may be presented here.

The teaching notes reveal that some concepts involved in the unit "Oxygen and Carbon Dioxide Cycle" were presented with great difficulty, especially on the lower grade levels. These concepts were: *oxygen, carbon dioxide, oxidation, reduction,* and the difference between *respiration* and *exchange of gases in food making.* It is evident that an understanding of these concepts is necessary to an understanding of the unit of which they are components.

The teaching notes indicate that some of these concepts were approached with less difficulty on the fourth, fifth, and sixth grade levels and the test results show that there was some comprehension of the meanings involved in these concepts on these higher grade levels. But the unit "Oxygen and Carbon Dioxide Cycle" proved to be one of the most difficult to teach on any of the levels studied, and the above considerations are presented as explanation.

The unit "Relation of Light to Animal Life (exclusive of mention of Plants as Intermediaries)" was not taught directly on the grade levels studied. Information pertaining to the unit reached the children as parts of several films that were shown and in other incidental ways. Thus may be explained the failure to learn what appears to be a rather simple unit.

As for the third unit "Comparison of Natural and Artificial Lights and Their Effect upon Plant Life," it should be noted that many children made such statements as "Electric light is not as good as sunlight for plants" or "Plants will grow in electric light," but the unit was held as being learned when a majority of the group gave explanations or reasons for the comparative effect of electric light and sunlight upon green plant life.

Some information bearing upon the difficulty encountered in teaching such reasons or explanations is taken from the teaching notes and the test data.

First of all, as mentioned elsewhere in this discussion, it was difficult to present the idea of the cross-section of the green leaf to the children of the lower grade levels. It seemed that the possession of this learning experience would facilitate the teaching of the unit "Comparison of Natural and Artificial Light and Their Effects upon Plant Life."

Then it was difficult to give an idea of differences in available power or energy of the various spectral colors of light even though children of the lower grade levels knew, or could rather easily be shown, that sunlight was composed of various "colors." However, on the higher grade levels the children had acquired some background of experience with ideas of *ultra-violet, infra-red, power of ultra-violet light,* etc., and connections were therefore made more readily in the instruction.

Finally, it seems that this particular unit could be taught and learned more readily if the children could be shown that ordinary electric light does not yield the same spectrum as sunlight. This could be told to the children but facilities for demonstration were not at hand.

Two of these three units were therefore not well learned, probably because of the difficulty in giving what seemed to be the necessary learning experiences. The third unit probably could have been presented and learned, but, because its component elements did not greatly contribute to an understanding of the integrating objective, the instruction concerning it was incidental.

IV. CORRELATION BETWEEN COMPLEXITY AND GRADE LEARNING

It may be well to emphasize here what has become apparent from the preceding discussion, viz., that those units which by the criteria of this study are classified as simple units were learned on the lower grade levels and those units classified as complex were learned on the higher grade levels.

Of the four simple units all were learned on the lower grade levels except one, viz., The Relation of Light to Animal Life (exclusive of mention of Plants as Intermediaries). As has been explained, this unit was presented only incidentally on all of the six grade levels.

Of the three complex units, the unit "Food and Fuel Making by Plants" was adequately approached only on the fourth, fifth, and sixth grade levels. The units "Oxygen and Carbon Dioxide Cycle" and "Comparison of Natural and Artificial Light" were not adequately learned on any of the six grade levels.

V. THE ERRORS OF THE UNITS

A consideration of erroneous statements made by the children, especially after instruction, contributes to interpretation of data.

When these statements are examined it is evident that some of them can be questioned as to their classification as absolute errors. For example, the statement "A plant in the dark gets dirty air and then gets yellow" is a definite error which admits of no possible interpretation as an ambiguity, or explanation as an unsuccessful expression of a correct idea which might have been held. But the statement "Plants make food out of air and water," while wrong, admits of question as an absolute error. For one thing, by substituting "from" or "with" for "out of," the statement becomes not entirely wrong, and it is possible that the child held a fairly correct idea but did not express it clearly—a license in interpretation which the first example does not permit. This ambiguous character of certain of the errors will therefore constitute the criterion of selection for the following presentation.

These gross errors will be presented and discussed under the various units of which they are a part. Although the post-instructional errors contribute more to an interpretation of the data, the pre-instructional errors are discussed at significant points.

Unit A. Necessities for Plant Growth and Life (exclusive of mention of Food and Fuel Making). There are no unambiguous errors concerning this unit.

Unit B. Effect of Light on Plants (exclusive of mention of Food and Fuel Making). In the first grades three children stated, after instruction, that plants bend to the window to get air. This was not a case of instruction imparting the erroneous idea, but rather the failure to change the false idea which was held, in four cases, before instruction.

One second grade child thought that plants get yellow in the dark because they get dirty air there and one sixth grade child thought that plants get yellow in the dark because they get no air.

There was one statement by a sixth grade child to the effect that sunlight contains chlorophyll. In the discussion of the errors of Unit F it is mentioned that this same idea occurred once on the fourth grade level in connection with the work of that unit.

Unit C. Interrelations of Plants and Animals (exclusive of mention of Oxygen and Carbon Dioxide Cycle). There are no unambiguous errors concerning this unit.

Unit D. Relation of Light to Animal Life (exclusive of mention of Plants as Intermediaries). There are no gross errors concerning this unit.

Unit E. Comparison of Natural and Artificial Light and Their Effects upon Plant Life. The only error of note concerning this unit is that sunlight has food in it. It is found in one case on the second grade level. (See the Food and Fuel Making Unit where the idea of plants obtaining food from sun and sunlight is quite common.)

Unit F. Food and Fuel Making by Plants. Where the Plant Gets Food. The error concerning this unit which is found throughout the greatest range of grade levels is that plants "get" their food from some outside source (dirt, people, water, air, sun, light, and fertilizer). It is very prevalent on the first and second grade levels but becomes less so on the third grade level. It is evidenced but once on the fourth grade level and not at all on the fifth and sixth grade levels. An error similar to this "getting" idea, found once in the third grade data, is that plants "eat" rain and dirt.

In a preceding discussion it was explained that this particular unit began to be learned by a majority of the pupils at the fourth grade level. Evidently the chief effect of instruction concerning this unit in the first three grades was to give the erroneous idea of "getting" food from air, water, sun, etc., rather than the more correct ideas concerning food making from, or with, these materials.

Another error, found twice on the second grade level, is that plants make food by "mixing" sun, dirt, and water. This "mixing" idea is found again, in three cases, on the fifth grade level, but here a refinement is given to the idea by the children saying that sunlight gives plants the "power" to "mix" the air and water to make food.

Two errors are made concerning the chlorophyll or "green bodies." Both errors are made on the fourth grade level. The first error, made once, is that chlorophyll comes from the sun. The second, made in five cases, is that light makes the little cells work like machines, thus "gathering up" the water, dirt, and air out of which the food is made.

Unit G. Oxygen and Carbon Dioxide Cycle. The Balanced Aquarium. The most frequent and the most persistent error concerned the distinction between respiration in green plants and the exchange of gases in the process of photosynthesis. Evidence of the failure to understand the difference between the two occurs on the first grade level where a child states that plants "breathe out" the "stuff" we breathe in and we breathe in "what" they breathe out. On the second grade level "bad air" and "good air" are used by three children as "stuff" was used in the first grades.

On the fourth grade level the term carbon dioxide is used but plants "breathe in carbon dioxide." Seven children thus express this idea.

The error then becomes less frequent on the fifth and sixth grade levels. It is found once in the fifth grades and twice in the sixth. Five sixth grade statements imply that plants breathe in carbon dioxide during the daytime but oxygen at night. The idea of plants "sucking up" the dirt in the fish bowl is found once in the first grades and twice in the second grades.

A first grade child thought that plants "eat" the water in the fish bowl, thus making it better for the fish and a second grade child thought that "dirty water goes into the plant and clean water comes out of it." On the fourth grade level it is stated once that "plants eat up the dirt."

A fourth grade child said that we breathe out oxygen and breathe in carbon dioxide.

VI. CORRELATION BETWEEN ERRORS, COMPLEXITY, AND GRADE LEARNING

A further correlation may now be emphasized in addition to that stated on page 94.

It will have been noted from the discussions of this chapter that not only is it the case that the simple units are learned on the lower grade levels and the complex units on the higher grade levels but also that the greater number of errors are made in connection with the complex units. These errors are made most frequently on the lower grade levels where the units are inadequately learned.

For but one of the four simple units are there any errors and they are few in number. This is the unit "Effect of Light on Plants (exclusive of mention of Food and Fuel Making)."

For two of the three complex units there are numerous errors. There are few errors for one of the complex units, viz., "Comparison of Natural and Artificial Lights and Their Effects upon Plant Life." It has been mentioned that it was difficult to present many learning experiences fundamental to this unit. Where there is little or no learning there are, of course, few errors made.

VII. GENERALIZATION AS A PROCESS OF THOUGHT

There is considerable discussion as to the place of generalization in child learning in science. But much of that which has been said concerning generalization leads to confusion because there are two types of generalization discussed and the two are not always distinguished. There are those who consider a generalization to be any of the statements referred to in this study as the objective type of aim. And there are others who refer to generalization as a statement of explanation of experience.

Dewey[3] says:

> Generalization is not a separate and single act; it is rather a constant tendency and function of the entire discussion or recitation. Every step forward toward an idea that comprehends, that explains, that unites what was isolated and therefore puzzling, generalizes. . . . The factor of formulation, of conscious stating, involved in generalization should also be a constant function, not a single formal act.

In the first sense the term refers to a product of mature thought —the present tentatively held end result of numberless explanations of all degrees of complexity and correctness, while in the second sense the term refers to a process or thought movement. In the case of this study this thought movement was directed toward an objective or end product of thought. In the case of all instruction organized on the basis of the objective the process of explanation will be directed toward such an end product. But, in this second sense, the learner is generalizing when there is explanation of experience. There is generalization not solely when the words of the objective are reproduced.

This distinction is very important, for with the advocacy of the objective as a guide to the organization of elementary school science instruction the question, Can children generalize? is constantly being raised:

Freeman[4] says:

> Another question is more fundamental. The Committee concludes from current psychological theory that the child's mental development is gradual rather than saltatory. From this it concludes a somewhat different principle, namely, that the child's mental operations are the same at various ages and that, therefore, the kind of scientific study which is appropriate is pre-

---

[3] Dewey, John, *How We Think.*

[4] Freeman, F. N., "Comments on the Program for Teaching Science from the Psychological Point of View." *Science Education*, Vol. 16, No. 4, p. 304, April, 1932.

cisely the same at all ages. In other words, generalizing should occupy as prominent a place in the study which the young child makes of the phenomena of the world about him as it does in the study carried on by older persons. I am not at all sure that this is the case. At any rate I do not believe we have enough evidence to make us sure of this sweeping conclusion. To the young child phenomena may be more nearly just phenomena—happenings. There may be more place for the wide-eyed watching of the drama of life without for the moment inquiring too deeply into its explanation.

The data of this study give abundant evidence that these children generalized, even in the lowest grades. A single example, running through the six grades, will be selected for illustration. The experience of observing the turning of a plant toward the light will be selected as an example of a happening or phenomenon and along with it will be given the most complex explanation or generalization made concerning it on each of the six grade levels.

The First Grades

Observation or Happening	*Generalization or Explanation*
Plants turn toward the window.	Plants turn to the window to get light because light makes them strong. Plants bend to the window to get light because they must stay green.

The Second Grades

Plants turn toward the window to get light.	Plants get yellow and die in the dark because they have no light to make food.

The Third Grades

Plants bend to the window to get light.	In the dark the plant would lose all of the food in it and then get yellow and die.

The Fourth Grades

Plants turn toward the sun.	If you put a plant in the dark it will not have green in its leaves because the little machines that make food for the plant stop working.

The Fifth Grade

The plant follows the sun.	A plant in the dark with plenty of good soil and water would never live unless it had been in the sunlight and had stored up a little food with which it could live for a while.

Plants turn toward the light.	The chlorophyll (or green color) in the leaves acts like a machine, and through the energy of the sun makes food which is stored in the stem and leaves of the plant.

Many other observations or happenings which are explained (i.e., many other illustrations of generalization) could be taken from the data. But the examples which are given show that these children generalized on all six of the grade levels studied. The generalizations which were made on the lower grade levels were less complex than those made on the higher grade levels, but the children generalized in terms of their experience. On the first grade level the generalization involved only the concept of *strength* or *green color*. On the second grade level *food making* appears. On the third grade level the concept of *food making* is associated with *food loss* and *change of color*. On the fourth grade level *green leaf* is associated with *little machines* and *food making*. On the fifth grade level to the concept *food making* are added *food storage* and function of *soil and water*. And on the sixth grade level concepts *chlorophyll, machines, sun energy, food making, food storage*, and *stem and leaf* are associated.

Frequent reference to these objective aims as "large generalizations" has undoubtedly contributed to the idea that generalization takes place only when these objectives are formulated by the learner. But when the emphasis is shifted to the conception of generalization as a continuous and progressive process of explanation contributory to such end products of thought, it is seen that the children of this study generalized on all of the grade levels. The difference between the mental operations of the children of the first and sixth grades was not one of ability to generalize but one concerning the complexity of generalizations.

The abundance and variety of explanation throughout the data of this study strongly indicate that the objective when it was stated was not repeated by rote. As one example, statements evidencing an attainment of the objective (awareness of energy transformation) are appreciably numerous only on those grade levels where knowledge of the process of food making (explanation) is evidenced.

CHAPTER X

Summary with Implications and Recommendations for Science Teachers and Curriculum Workers

1. STATEMENTS excerpted from an extensive survey of the literature in the field of elementary school science instruction bring into relief five well-defined issues. These issues have become crystallized into two different philosophies of science instruction which are based upon different psychological assumptions. This study was made in order to secure experimental data bearing upon certain basic assumptions of one of these philosophies of science instruction.

2. One assumption of the philosophy tested is that its application necessitates particular kinds of mental processes. Another is that young children are capable of these mental processes. The study contributes experimental data bearing upon the kind of mental process which is thus involved and tests its possibilities and characteristics with children of the first six grades of an elementary school.

3. A third assumption of the philosophy tested is that a practical gradation can be effected by use of the objective type of aim. The study contributes experimental data bearing upon the possibilities and characteristics of such a continuous gradation by use of the objective type of aim.

4. The survey of the professional literature reveals two other proposals for gradation of content. One is that the aim used on the lower grade levels shall differ from that used on the higher grade levels (aesthetic aims on the lower grade levels and economic aims on the higher grade levels). Another is that gradation shall be made in terms of the division of science from which the content is taken (from the biological sciences on the lower grade levels and from the physical sciences on the higher levels).

5. An objective for experimental study is selected after a survey of studies in the field of science education and of needs in science teaching. This objective is made more definitive by the formula-

tion and application of two postulatory criteria, the validity of which is later demonstrated upon the basis of an analysis of statements written by authorities for the non-specialist reader and an analysis of statements made by elementary school children.

6. How the objective type of aim is indicative of the learning experiences necessary for its approach and attainment is demonstrated. When the teacher of science encounters an aim stated thus: "Green plants convert the energy of light into the energy of food and fuel," there is definitive suggestion as to what the teaching is to be about. Although different teachers will not select and present the identical content in the identical manner, the desired outcome of the instruction is clearly and unambiguously stated and the teacher has an indication of the content required for its attainment or treatment. It is pointed out that such is not the case with such statements of aims as "spirituality," "moral uprightness," and the like, or with aims stated as they are in many courses of study, such as "plants," "garden truck." It may properly be asked, what is to be taught about "plants" or "garden truck" and what is to be used to teach "spirituality" and "moral uprightness"?

7. By use of the objective type of aim the teacher can test for and verify various degrees of attainment of the aim. Attainment of such aims as "spirituality," "steadfastness," "moral uprightness," and the like through science instruction is highly desirable, but so far it has not been demonstrated how their approximation may be verified.

8. The same objective can be used to select elements of learning for presentation throughout a range of grade levels. All of these contributory elements may not be learned on every grade level but some of them will be learned on each grade level. The learning depends upon the complexity of the elements. The complexity of the elements depends upon (1) the number of concepts associated and (2) the number and immediacy of the experiences which are involved in the concepts associated. Thus, since the same objective can be used to select a progressively complex array of elements and since some portion of the array can be learned on every grade level, gradation by use of the objective type of aim is not only possible but to be recommended as a plan corresponding with the method of learning.

9. The use of the objective type of aim does not necessitate its statement on every grade level. The same objective is, however,

to be held by the teacher on all grade levels. The learning experiences which were given to the first grade children of this study were selected and interpreted with the objective in mind, but the objective was not stated on this grade level. Nevertheless, the objective was functioning as a means to selection, interpretation, and gradation of content which was both worth while in itself and ultimately contributory to the objective.

10. When the objective type of aim is used, the "same kind of learning" is not to be expected from the children of all grade levels. The data of this study show that the learning of the children of the lower grade levels differed from that of the higher grade levels. They show that the differences are due to the complexity of association of concepts and the complexity of the experiences involved in the concepts associated. The learning on both low and high grade levels is, however, characterized by the association of ideas gained from experiences and in this there is no difference. But there is a difference in the complexity of the associations and it is this difference which gives the key to a plan for rational gradation.

11. The data indicate the presence of the same kind of mental activity on all of the grade levels studied. The grade differences are found in the complexity of the product of these mental activities.

12. An "understanding of an objective" is not approached or secured through repetition of the same or similar words of the objective but through the interpretation of numerous and varied learning experiences in such terms of the objective as are possible with the particular grade level.

13. Two senses in which the term "generalization" is used in the field of science instruction are distinguished. It is proposed that the term be applied to a process or thought movement rather than to a statement of thought product. The data of this study indicate that the children generalized in all six of the grade levels studied. Illustrations are given to show that this process was in terms of their experience.

14. It is suggested that verbalism or memorization of the objective of instruction may be controlled in teaching and detected in learning by attention to the amount and type of the generalization or explanation contributory to the objective. There is selected for illustration one of numerous arrays of explanatory statements

found in the data of this study which indicate that true understanding of the objective of this instruction was approached and that the objective, when stated, was not rote reproduction.

15. A definition and construction of units determined upon the basis of the objective type of aim is presented. This organization is based clearly and directly upon considerations of the method of child learning.

16. It is suggested that further study on higher grade levels of the objective here treated would yield information bearing upon questions involved in the beginnings of specialization and the attainment of understanding of broad objectives.

17. When the objective type of aim is used in instruction the learner's pre-instructional ideas pertaining to the objective which is to be presented should be ascertained as fully and exactly as possible. Indications are thus furnished concerning ideas from which the instruction may proceed, and vague and erroneous ideas which are held before instruction will be more certainly changed by the instruction. The data show, however, that in several cases the erroneous ideas held before instruction were not changed by the instruction.

18. On the lower grade levels, when relatively complex ideas were presented the instruction had the effect of imparting, not vaguely correct ideas which might be utilized in progression toward an understanding of the objective, but an appreciable number of decidedly erroneous ideas.

19. There is a function to be attained through the use of the objective type of aim which is not so clearly demonstrated in this study but the evidence of which might have been conspicuous had the study been organized about some other objective. It is that the content contributory to an understanding of the objective can be selected from all fields of science. It has been shown that some of those interested in elementary school science instruction recommend the biological sciences for the lower grade levels and the physical sciences for the higher grade levels. Distinction in the field of subject matter is in this case the criterion of grade placement. When the objective type of aim is used, the criterion of grade placement is complexity of learning experiences, irrespective of the fields of science from which these experiences are taken. There is no experimental evidence that content from the biological sciences is less difficult for children than content from the physical

sciences and therefore better adapted to the lower grade levels of the elementary school.

20. An analysis of statements made by authorities for the non-specialist reader concerning *light* shows that light is discussed in relation to a considerable range of topics. The discussion of its relation to energy and its transformations ranks second in number of statements. And more is said concerning the energy relations of light to life, particularly to plant life, than concerning any other energy relation of light.

21. An analysis of statements concerning light made by elementary school children shows that these children thought of light in connection with a wide range of phenomena, chief among which were phenomena of energy transfer. Elementary school teachers, when considering the topic of *light* for presentation to children, should realize that it possesses richer possibilities than are displayed in the development of the topic which is given in the usual high school or college course in physics. It would be well to show, by similar techniques, some of the relations of other topics which are often considered too narrowly by teachers of science on all grade levels.

Bibliography

A. PSYCHOLOGY AND PROCEDURE

BAGLEY, W. C. Educational Values. The Macmillan Co., 1912.

BAGLEY, W. C. The Educative Process. The Macmillan Co., 1920.

BALDWIN, J. M. Handbook of Psychology. Henry Holt and Co., 1890.

BALDWIN, J. M. Mental Development in the Child and the Race. The Macmillan Co., 1900.

BILLIG, F. G. A Technique for Developing Content for a Professional Course in Science for Teachers in Elementary Schools. Bureau of Publications, Teachers College, Columbia University, 1930.

BLACK, O. F. The Development of Certain Concepts of Physics in High School Students. Die Wiste, Potchefstroom, South Africa, 1930. (Distributed through A. G. Seiler, New York City.)

BROWN, H. W. Some Records of the Thoughts and Reasonings of Children. Pedagogical Seminary, Vol. II, pp. 358-96, 1892.

CAMERON, E. H. Condensation of Experience. A Cyclopedia of Education, Vol. II, pp. 173-174. The Macmillan Co., 1911.

CASE, A. Children's Ideas of God. Religious Education, Vol. xvi, No. 3, pp. 143-146, June, 1921.

CHAMBERS, W. G. How Words Get Meaning. The Pedagogical Seminary. Vol. XI, No. 1, pp. 30-50, March, 1904.

CRAIG, G. S. Certain Techniques Used in Developing a Course of Study in Science for the Horace Mann Elementary School. Bureau of Publications, Teachers College, Columbia University, 1927.

DEWEY, JOHN. Reasoning in Early Childhood. Teachers College Record, Vol. XV, pp. 9-15, 1914.

DEWEY, JOHN. Generalization. A Cyclopedia of Education, Vol. III, p. 15. The Macmillan Co., 1912.

DEWEY, JOHN. Concrete and Abstract. A Cyclopedia of Education, Vol. II, p. 173. The Macmillan Co., 1911.

DEWEY, JOHN. Conception. A Cyclopedia of Education, Vol. II, pp. 171-172. The Macmillan Co., 1911.

DEWEY, JOHN. How We Think. D. C. Heath and Co., 1910.

DUNLAP, KNIGHT. The Elements of Scientific Psychology, pp. 162-164. C. V. Mosby Co., 1922.

FREEMAN, F. N. Thirty-First Yearbook of the National Society for the Study of Education, Part I. Public School Publishing Co., 1932.

FREEMAN, F. N. A Symposium on the Thirty-First Yearbook of the National Society for the Study of Education. Part I. Entitled, "A Program for Teaching Science." Science Education, Vol. 16, No. 4, April, 1932.

GATES, A. I. Psychology for Students of Education. The Macmillan Co., 1923.

HALL, G. S. The Contents of Children's Minds on Entering School. E. L. Kellogg and Co., 1893.

ISAACS, SUSAN. Intellectual Growth in Young Children. Harcourt, Brace and Co., 1930.

LATON, A. D. The Psychology of Learning Applied to Health Education through Biology. Bureau of Publications, Teachers College, Columbia University, 1929.

LEUBA, J. H. Children's Conceptions of God and Religious Education. Religious Education, Vol. XII, No. 1, pp. 5-15, February, 1917.

LUCKEY, G. W. A. The Essentials of Child Study. University Publishing Co., 1917.

MACKAY, MINNETTE. The Formation of a Generalization in the Minds of Ninth Grade Biology Students. Doctor's dissertation (manuscript), Teachers College, Columbia University, New York, 1930.

MACLEAN, A. H. The Idea of God in Protestant Religious Education. Bureau of Publications, Teachers College, Columbia University, 1930.

McDONOUGH, A. R. The Development of Meaning. Psychological Monographs, XXVII, 1919.

MELTZER, H. Children's Social Concepts. Bureau of Publications, Teachers College, Columbia University, 1925.

PARKER, S. C. Methods of Teaching in High Schools. Ginn & Co., 1915.

PIAGET, J. The Child's Conception of Physical Causality. Harcourt, Brace and Co., 1930.

PIAGET, J. The Child's Conception of the World. Harcourt, Brace and Co., 1929.

PIAGET, J. The Language and Thought of the Child. Harcourt, Brace and Co., 1926.

PILLSBURY, W. B. The Essentials of Psychology. The Macmillan Co., 1920.

POWERS, S. R. Research in Science Teaching. Teachers College Record, Vol. XXX, No. 4, pp. 334-342, January, 1929.

POWERS, S. R. Educational Values of Science Teaching. Teachers College Record, Vol. XXXII, No. 1, pp. 17-33, October, 1930.

POWERS, S. R. A Program for Teaching Science. National Society for the Study of Education. Thirty-First Yearbook, Part I. Public School Publishing Co., 1932.

ROUSSEAU, J. J. Émile. (D. Appleton and Co.; originally published 1762.)

SPEARMAN, C. The Nature of Intelligence and the Principles of Cognition. The Macmillan Co., 1923.

Studies in Education (Edited by Earl Barnes). How Words Get Content. Vol. I, No. 2, pp. 43-61, 1902.

TAYLOR, G. A. An Inventory of the Minds of Individuals of Six and Seven Years Mental Age. Bureau of Publications, Teachers College, Columbia University, 1923.

THORNDIKE, E. L. The Elements of Psychology. A. G. Seiler, 1905.

THORNDIKE, E. L. Notes on Child Study. The Macmillan Co., 1903.

TITCHENER, E. B. Lectures on the Experimental Psychology of the Thought Processes. The Macmillan Co., 1909.

WOODBRIDGE, F. J. E. Empiricism. A Cyclopedia of Education. Vol. II, pp. 442-444. The Macmillan Co., 1912.

WOODWORTH, R. S: Imageless Thought. The Journal of Philosophy, Psychology, and Scientific Methods, Vol. III, pp. 701-708, 1906.

B. SCIENCE CONTENT

For Adults

BAZZONI, C. B. Kernels of the Universe. George H. Doran Co., 1927.

BERGSON, H. Creative Evolution. Henry Holt and Co., 1911.

BOWER, F. O. Plants and Man. The Macmillan Co., 1925.

CLARKE, B. L. Romance of Reality. The Macmillan Co., 1928.

DEMING, H. G. In the Realm of Carbon. John Wiley and Sons, Inc., 1930.

HEYL, P. R. Fundamental Concepts of Physics in the Light of Modern Discovery. Williams and Wilkins Co., 1926.

JOHNSTONE, J. The Mechanism of Life. Longmans, Green and Co., 1921.

JOHNSTONE, J. The Philosophy of Biology. Harvard University Press, 1914.

LEWIS, G. N. Anatomy of Science. Yale University Press, 1927.

NEWMAN, H. H. Nature of the World and of Man. University of Chicago Press, 1926.

SLOSSON, E. E. Snapshots of Science. Century Co., 1928.

SODDY, FREDERICK. Matter and Energy. Henry Holt and Co., 1912.

For Children

MACDOUGALL, D. T. The Green Leaf. D. Appleton and Co., 1930.

The Book of Popular Science. The Energy of Plants, Vol. 5, pp. 1577-1582. The Grolier Society.

C. PHILOSOPHY AND ORGANIZATION OF NATURE STUDY AND ELEMENTARY SCHOOL SCIENCE

BAILEY, L. H. The Nature Study Idea. The Macmillan Co., 1911.

BIGELOW, M. A. The Established Principles of Nature Study. Nature Study Review, Vol. 3, pp. 1-7, 1907.

BIGELOW, M. A. Some Fundamental Propositions for Nature Study. Nature Study Review, Vol. 11, pp. 410-412, 1915.

COULTER, S., HODGE, C. F., MANN, C. R. The Relation of Nature Study and Science Teaching. Nature Study Review, Vol. 4, pp. 10-24, 1908.

CRAIG, G. S. Science for the Elementary School Child. Child Study, Vol. 6, pp. 208-211, 1929.

CRAIG, G. S. Certain Techniques Used in Developing a Course of Study in Science for the Horace Mann Elementary School. Bureau of Publications, Teachers College, Columbia University, 1927.

DEPARTMENT OF SUPERINTENDENCE. Fourth Yearbook. The Nation at Work on the Public School Curriculum. Washington, D. C., 1926.

DOWNING, E. R. The Nature Study Course. Nature Study Review, Vol. 3, pp. 191-195, 1907.

Bibliography

GANONG, W. F.   Nature Courses and Science Courses.   Nature Study Review, Vol. 4, pp. 242-246, 1908.

HODGE, C. F.   Nature Study and Life.   Ginn & Co., 1902.

HOLTZ, F. L.   Nature Study.   Charles Scribner's Sons, 1908.

JACKMAN, W. S.   Nature Study for the Common Schools.   Henry Holt and Co., 1894.

JACKMAN, W. S.   Nature Study.   Third Yearbook of the National Society for the Study of Education, Part II.   Public School Publishing Co., 1904.

JACKMAN, W. S.   Nature Study and Related Subjects for the Common Schools.   Part II.   Notes.   Published by the Author, 1896.

MUNSON, J. P.   Education through Nature Study.   E. L. Kellogg and Co., 1903.

NATIONAL SOCIETY FOR THE STUDY OF EDUCATION.   Thirty-First Yearbook, Part I.   Public School Publishing Co., 1932.

PACK, A. N., and PALMER, E. L.   The Nature Almanac.   The American Nature Association, 1927.

TRAFTON, G. H.   The Teaching of Science in the Elementary School.   Houghton Mifflin Co., 1918.

WOODHULL, J. F.   Physical Nature Study.   Nature Study Review, Vol. 6, pp. 5-10, 1910.

D. MISCELLANEOUS

American Men of Science.   The Science Press, 1927.

Book Review Digest.   The H. W. Wilson Co., 1925-1929.